Electric Graffiti

To friends and family

Electric Graffiti

GUS SILBER

Musings on a Facebook Wall

BOOK**STORM**

ISBN: 978-1-928257-71-4
e-ISBN: 978-1-928257-72-1

First edition, first impression 2020

Published by Bookstorm (Pty) Ltd
PO Box 4532
Northcliff 2115
Johannesburg
South Africa

www.bookstorm.co.za

Every effort has been made to trace copyright holders and to obtain their
permission for the use of copyright material. The publisher apologises for
any errors or omissions and would be grateful if notified of any corrections
that should be incorporated in future reprints or editions of this book.

Edited by Kelly Norwood-Young
Proofread by Jennifer Malec
Photographs supplied by author, unless otherwise indicated
Cover design by mr design
Book design and typesetting by Triple M Design
Emojis courtesy of Shutterstock
Printed in the USA

Contents

Foreword: Dispatches from an invisible country

If you were to set off from your home one fine morning, and you took a few steps towards the horizon, and then a few more, and then a few more and more, you will, so the theory goes, eventually find yourself right back where you started. You will have circumnavigated the globe, even if your intention was merely to go for a quick stroll.

Certainly, you would have had to fjord a few rivers and sail a few seas along the way, and at the border, you would have had to make sure that your papers were in order. But you would be home, and as TS Eliot put it, after all your ceaseless exploration, you would know the place for the first time.

By the same sort of process, a few years ago, I wrote a few words and posted them to Facebook, and then a few more, and a few more. And today I find, to my surprise, that I have accidentally written a book.

It was Louise Grantham of the Bookstorm publishing company who first pointed this out to me, and my immediate reaction was, really? A book? I had no idea. The moving finger writes; and having writ, moves on, wrote Omar Khayyam, and he could have been talking about social media in the 21st century.

On Twitter we call it a stream, a restless rush of news and views and observations and asides and quips and snips and volleys and retorts. (I like to drop anchor and watch these miniature battles; they're like ping-pong, played with poison darts.) On Facebook we call it a feed, a buffet of dispatches served on a conveyer belt, in answer to the age-old question: what's on your mind?

Either way, they come and they go, and rarely do we pause to look back on the road we have travelled. So thank you, first of all, Louise, for taking the huge trouble of combing through my back-posts and setting the idea in stone.

The defining material of our age is a much more fragile fabric: the ether of information, like flash paper that ignites or crumbles to dust at our touch. What would happen if it fell into the wrong hands?

I am, naïvely, a utopian when it comes to the internet, a technology that was first finessed in the Pentagon and designed for use during wartime. The fact that we now deploy it, day by day, to let people know what's happening and what's on our minds, is in its own way, a tribute to the quiet triumph of humanism.

The great promise of the social networks, on the borderless, invisible country of the internet, is that they can provide a space for humans to be human. And what are we other than vessels for emotion in motion, moving forward one step at a time, on a journey of ceaseless exploration that will lead us right back to where we started, so that we can know the place for the first time.

The journey begins here. Thank you for joining me.

@gussilber
Johannesburg
January 2020

Thank yous

Thank you, Louise Grantham, Russell Clarke, Nicola van Rooyen, and the rest of the team at Bookstorm, for shepherding this book from the concept to the printed page. Thank you, Kelly Norwood-Young, for your expert and insightful editing – I am actually quite fond of dashes, after all! Thank you, Marius Roux, for the very cool cover design.

Thank you to my siblings across the waters, Rhoda, Elaine, and Harold, for reading and chatting from so far, and yet so near.

Thank you, at home, to Amanda, for reading my posts with a very fine eye and an occasional sigh, and to Sarah-Jane, Max, and Rachel for graciously agreeing to make guest appearances in my posts, and for reading them too, even though they are 'way too long'. (Sorry, I didn't have time to write them short, as we like to say in the writing-and-posting business.)

Thank you, Mark Zuckerberg, above all, for the editing function in Facebook, a generous accommodation of human frailty, that I can only hope Twitter will one day imitate. And thank you, too, to friends, followers, fellow citizens of the invisible country of the internet, for the conversations, the inspirations, the sharing, and the community.

'Bohemian Rhapsody' and the Prince of Denmark

A few years ago, out of a sense of neighbourly obligation and morbid curiosity, I attended an amateur talent evening at a local church hall.

There was a piano recital, played with an air of studious grace; there was a stand-up comedian, with some wry and cutting observations on race and suburbia; there was a dancer doing a jazz routine, with a smile on her face and her feet all over the place.

Then it was the turn of a rock band, a three-piece in the classic format of drums, bass, and guitar. They looked shy and earnest – it must have been their first gig – and as the guitarist leaned back and strummed the opening power chord, there was a squeal and a fritz as the amp cut out, leaving just a shiver of steel strings scratching at the air.

The band convened to analyse the problem, fiddling with the dials and trouble-checking the connections, and the MC rushed on stage and said, this won't take a minute, and she was right.

She stood there for a while, looking on and smiling as the minutes ticked by, and then, out of nowhere, as if thinking aloud, she opened her mouth and sang: 'Is this the real life …'

On the other end of the stage, another member of the church's youth group answered the call, singing: 'Is this just fantasy?'

And someone in the audience, without any prompting, sang, 'Caught in a landslide,' and someone else sang, 'No escape from reality.'

And on and on, the thread of the a cappella rising in surge and volume, until we were all singing, all of us, the kids and the teens and the adults, all the way through the Scaramouch and the Fandango and the Galileo and the Mama Mia to the wistful ache of the fade-out – 'Any way the wind blows' – and the rapturous burst of self-applause that followed.

It was further proof, if any were needed, that everyone knows 'Bohemian Rhapsody', which was recorded by Queen in 1975, and which has since, thanks to its ubiquitous use in movies and ads and football stadium singalongs, become a bridge between the generations, a shared gene implanted in our collective cultural memory.

We all know the words of the song by heart, and yet their meaning remains mysterious, elusive, open to interpretation. But that is part of the beauty of art. Once the artist sets it free, it belongs to us all, and we can weigh it up and peel away its secrets in any way we choose.

So the way I hear it, and I'm hearing it a lot these days, in the hype-up to the release of the biopic of the same name, 'Bohemian Rhapsody' is about, well, six minutes long, during the course of which Freddie Mercury contemplates the most cosmic question of them all, on the mercurial nature of existence itself, the state of being or not being in the everyday world.

It's about the ancient, perpetual battle between the fates and the furies, between the tempests that rage all around us, and our innate drive to rise up and rage back against them.

If this sounds familiar, it's because the song can be heard as a modern riff on the most famous meditation on mortality in the English language: the fourth soliloquy from Shakespeare's *Hamlet*.

When the Prince of Denmark ponders whether to be or not to be, he is foreshadowing the anguish of Mercury's schizophrenic couplet, 'I don't wanna die,' followed immediately by 'I sometimes wish I'd never been born at all.'

And when Mercury moans, 'Too late, my time has come, sends

shivers down my spine, body's aching all the time,' he brings to mind Hamlet's meanderings on the 'heartache, and the thousand natural shocks that flesh is heir to'.

Hamlet, troubled out of his mind by his mom and dad, the latter who is a ghost, the former who married his dad's murderer with unseemly haste, is a tragic figure, bent on revenge and wallowing in self-pity, just as Freddie does when he cries: 'I'm just a poor boy, nobody loves me.'

Over the centuries, Hamlet's mental state has provided rich pickings for professional and amateur analysts alike: at the very least, he is melancholic, delusional and paranoid, with moments of crystal clarity and insight: 'When the wind is southerly,' he insists, 'I know a hawk from a handsaw.'

But it is worth remembering that Hamlet, too, must admit to his mama at one point that he killed a man, albeit the wrong man, and albeit with a sword thrust through a curtain, rather than a gun against the head.

Alas, poor Polonius, and alas all the others of royal ilk who – spoiler alert – are led to their untimely demise by the time the curtain falls.

'Bohemian Rhapsody' may have less drama to its plotting, but it has no less melodrama, and Freddie too veers from existential despair – 'nothing really matters anymore' – to the mania of the middle section, where he sees a little silhouetto of a man and gets very very frightened by the thunder and lightning.

Then he rages: 'So you think you can stone me and spit in my eye, so you think you can love me and leave me to die,' perhaps against a treacherous lover, perhaps against the universe; it's hard to tell and it's better that we don't know for sure.

It's enough that this song, this radical, audacious, format-defying work of pop genius, delves so deeply into a sea of troubles, and then takes arms against them with slings and arrows and drums and guitars, until the music itself becomes reason enough for being.

The lesson that lingers, as the final harmony fades into the ether, is this: in the battle between the fates and the furies, choose the furies.

Choose art, choose beauty, choose truth, choose life, choose to sing along to the words you know by heart, any way the wind blows.

Mxed agenda

Last week, Wits University announced that it was adding a new honorific to the list of options for internal correspondence with staff and students.

Along with the customary Mr, Mrs, Miss, and Ms, one can now choose to be addressed by the gender-neutral prefix, Mx, pronounced Mix.

Which actually is not that new, with the first recorded usage dating as far back as 1977, when the American magazine *Single Parent* carried a short story featuring the following exchange at a dinner party: 'On second thought, maybe both sexes should be called Mx. That would solve the gender problem entirely.'

Other languages have managed to solve this conundrum with elegant etiquette, the most notable being Japanese, where the standard formal form of address simply appends San to one's family name.

San is neither masculine nor feminine, so it can be used with impunity even if you are corresponding with someone whose gender or gender identity is not known to you.

We do have gender-neutral titles in English, Comrade, but they tend to be restricted to the professions: a Dr is a doctor, a Prof. is a professor, an Adv. is an advocate, and so on. Other than that, it's traditionally been a perpetual grapple.

I remember, as a starting-out journalist, the socially awkward agony of having to ask an interviewee whether they were a Mrs or a Miss, because newspaper style dictated a formality of usage that was almost feudal in its impertinence. I mean, really, especially when you consider that Mr is short for Master, and Mrs for Mistress.

Worse than that, you had to ask every interviewee their age, at which point the interview would often come to a bumbling, eye-widening halt.

And then there was the bizarre convention in court reporting, where an accused in a case would be identified by their honorific throughout ('Mr Charles Manson'), until and unless they were convicted, and then, with the awful finality of a guillotine, the honorific would be cleaved from their person and they would become plain Manson in your story.

Thankfully, nowadays, the vast majority of publications just call people by their surnames, whatever their status in life, which is a lot more democratic and un-stuffy.

The New York Times, the standard-bearer of formal journalistic style, still uses honorifics – 'Mr Keith Richards' – and uses Ms across the board for women. Ms has never really caught on in South Africa, for some reason.

I can only recall using it out loud in public once. That was at a press conference held by Whoopi Goldberg, who was shooting *Sarafina* in the country at the time.

There is no point going to a press conference if you are not prepared to stand up and embarrass yourself in front of your fellow hacks, so at some point I stood up, after carefully weighing my options. 'Whoopi' seemed way too informal and cosy, all the more so since the genesis of the nickname was an actual whoopee cushion; Mrs Goldberg would have been both technically inaccurate and stuffy; and as for Miss Goldberg, well, forget it.

So I stood up and said 'Ms Goldberg', and she smiled sweetly and answered my question in that gorgeous raspy drawl of hers, and then I went back home and wrote my story and just plain called her Whoopi.

The amazing bionic teenager

Today, at the SingularityU South Africa Summit in Kyalami, Johannesburg, I had the pleasure of meeting Tilly Lockey, whose topic of discussion, in conversation with Dr Benjamin Rosman, a computer scientist and AI and robotics researcher, was: 'What's Possible in the Future'.

It was with some trepidation that I reached out to shake Tilly's hand, because she had just been demonstrating her four levels of sensor-activated grip onstage, and I've seen what happens in the movies when people with bionic limbs – I'm thinking specifically of Darth Vader and Robocop here – activate their sensors and tighten their grip. But I needn't have worried.

Tilly is 14 years old, and her 3D-printed myoelectric arms, which are manufactured by Open Bionics in Bristol, England, are modelled on those of her action-movie hero, Alita the Battle Angel, an avenging cyborg warrior with a human brain.

Tilly's arms were a gift from the movie studio 20th Century Fox, and as she told me, up-turning her hands and looking at them, 'I love these hands. I wear them every single day.'

I could hear a faint whirring sound, akin to that made by robots when they articulate their joints, and I asked Tilly: 'Is that noise your …' She smiled and nodded, and she flexed her silver-grey fingers on the table. 'Whirr-whirr,' they whirred.

I noticed the scuffs and scratches on her arms, signs of the everyday wear caused by machines being put to good use, and Tilly, disarmingly, slipped one of her arms off and handed it to me.

I weighed its heft – about the same as an iPad – and I could see the sensor buttons on the inside.

A blue light glowed like a jewel on the top of the hand, and on the knuckles, there were claw-like projections that reminded me of Wolverine's slashing blades.

I thought of the gods of the Marvel universe, the superheroes who, beneath their skin and armour, are as human as you or I. Tilly slipped the arm back onto her stump. A Battle Angel, suiting up.

'I want lasers, torches, a Bluetooth speaker,' she said, mulling over the possibilities for the next generation of her bionic devices.

Tilly, who lives in Newcastle upon Tyne in the northeast of England, was just 15 months old when she contracted meningo-coccal septicaemia, a bacterial infection with a high mortality rate. To save her life, doctors had to amputate both her arms, just below the elbow.

As a toddler, she was fitted with prosthetic hands, supplied by the National Health Service, and they were almost medieval in their makeshift functionality: tubes with rudimentary finger-hooks, tied with elastic bands, the whole contraption controlled by a harness strapped around her back and shoulders.

'It was more of a weapon than a hand,' she says. 'I was trauma-tised by it.'

Later, she graduated to a pair of myoelectric limbs, powered by the natural electrical signals of the muscles, complete with freckles and paintable nails. But they were too realistic for comfort.

'People would look at me with, I don't want to say disgust, but confusion,' she says. 'They would avoid speaking to me. I would rather you came up to me and let me tell you my story.'

At school, her classmates were wowed by her Open Bionics arms, with their two-tone cyberpunk design: 'They kept wanting to shake my hand and stuff,' she says.

She thinks of her bionics as fashion accessories, not just medical devices: 'They're like a handbag or a pair of shoes. They're so customisable.'

Tilly has since become an ambassador for Open Bionics, as well as a beta-tester, consultant, and occasional inventor, her most practical contribution to date being a 'freeze mode' to clench the hand in place when required.

On her YouTube channel, she runs makeup tutorials, preferring to apply her makeup with one arm on and one arm off. I asked Tilly, who describes herself as 'an influencer, a blogger, a model, just your average 14-year-old girl, but with some pretty cool hands', what her arms and hands have taught her about life. (It's a question, I suppose, that could just as easily be asked of those of us whose arms and hands are fixed in place.) She mulled it over for a moment.

'I've learned that you don't have to be this, like, perfect person to do what you want in life,' she said. 'No matter what you're going through, you can still have success, if you just have the mindset that you can do what you want to do if you just go for it.'

And from Tilly Lockey today, I learned what's possible in the future, if we look upon it as an age when humans don't turn into machines, but when machines help us to become more human.

The agony of being inappropriately dressed in Cape Town

I have been laid low this week by a terrible bout of manfluenza, the direct result of an ill-advised exercise I undertook in Cape Town on Saturday.

Not that there is anything wrong, per se, about participating in the 5 km parkrun in the beautiful surrounds of Green Point Park, with its lush indigenous gardens, its magnificent views of the embracing crags and hillocks, and its gentle ponds on which waterfowl bob and seagulls belly-bomb.

Rather, the clue to my cluelessness came with the pre-run briefing, held in the whisk of a mild gust and the shiver of incipient drizzle.

The race organiser stood on his little box, as people warm-upped all around him, and he said, 'There is no such thing as cold in Cape Town. There is only inappropriate clothing.'

I had noticed, already, that almost everyone was wisely sealed in Gore-Tex, Lycra, and double layers of breathable, sweat-wicking cotton, while I, from Joburg, was wearing flimsy run-shorts, an FNB racing shirt, and takkies.

One of the key cultural differences between Johannesburg and Cape Town is that Capetonians have an almost psychic connection to the shifting, mercurial moods that shape and mould their city, and they are thus able to dress appropriately for a Fairest-Cape day, a Cape-of-Storms day, a raging southeaster, a searing heat-wave, or a run in the park in the rain.

Caught between the brazen barriers of mountain and ocean, they are able to intuit the weather to the merest degree, and this sixth sense allows them to take every day in their stride.

There was a man standing next to the race organiser, and he was holding a plastic ice-cream tub in his hands. At first I thought it was for harvesting rainwater, but it turned out to be for storing your car-keys while you ran.

I thought about it for a moment – handing my car-keys, complete with Airbnb keys, to a total stranger – but the cultural difference was too vast for me, so I clutched them in my hand as it started to rain and we started to run.

Back home the next day, the snivels started, gradually and then suddenly, confining me to bed with groaning, forehead-clutching, and the periodic popping of placebos from the chemist.

As if that wasn't enough, there was another shadow of Cape Town that had followed me to Joburg, and that was the warning, via WhatsApp group, of a widespread outage of water, caused by a substation fire.

The aquapocalypse was about to arrive, and for the first time, I felt prepared for it – 'paraat', to use the whip-smart Afrikaans term – thanks to the JoJo tank that had hitherto been gathering dust in the kitchen.

It's a small, sturdy tank, khaki in colour, 20 litres in capacity, meant for taking along on camping trips. (It can apparently also be used for storing wine, but I haven't tried that yet.)

As I filled it up for emergency supply, it struck me how the JoJo, which is one of the three great South African water-centric innovations, the other two being the Kreepy Krauly and the break-water dolos, has become associated with the ethos of frugality and conservationism by which Capetonians, in my experience, still devoutly abide.

The only complaint I heard from my Cape Town friends last week was that the cost of municipal water has risen dramatically, as a direct consequence of them saving so much water that the council now has to charge more to make up for the deficit. Talk about no good deed going unpunished.

But there is much we can learn, us JoJoburgers up here, from those Capetonians down below, and the next time I find myself in the Mother City on a Saturday morning, I am going to make extra sure that I am appropriately dressed for the occasion.

And the cars look very different today

What a moment today has been in the history of the planet we call home. Somewhere above our heads, thousands of kilometres high, floats a speck of grit in the canvas of the heavens: a gleaming cherry-red Tesla Roadster with alloy wheels, and in the driver's seat, arm casually slung over the window, sits a mannequin in a space suit, a proxy for the entire human race and how far we have travelled.

The sign on the dashboard reads DON'T PANIC!, the panicky injunction from the opening book of *The Hitchhiker's Guide to the Galaxy*, and on the stereo, in an infinite loop, 'Space Oddity' by David Bowie is playing, over and over and over again.

In space, of course, there is no sound, just the eternal stillness of eternal night, so I put the song on Google Play while I watched the livestream of the first car in orbit; the payload of Elon Musk's monster rocket, the Falcon Heavy, which in itself is a sly, school-boyish pun for the size and capability of the beast, with its 27 engines generating five-million pounds of thrust at takeoff. It's so Falcon Heavy, man.

On one level, this voyage, ostensibly a test flight, is the most audacious marketing stunt ever performed on or off the earth, but on another, there was something deep and sublime about the trajectory of this flying car, cruising in the silent void where we don't need roads.

'For here am I, sitting in a tin can, far above the world,' sang David Bowie, as the reflection of the small blue planet oozed like a globule of mercury along the glossy red curves of the convertible, and a burst of sun cast a flare into the blackness.

Far below the Tesla, lay earth, aswirl with clouds, the planet of war and madness and the venality of politicians, but the planet, too, of hope and love and wonder, and the genius of scientists and engineers who conceive the impossible, and then touch a button to count it down on a plume of fire into space.

The roadster is on its way now to the asteroid belt, between the orbits of Jupiter and Mars, where it will wander, says Elon Musk, for a billion years. And if any other species out there happens to chance upon it, what will they think of us?

That we are a race of dreamers, that we can build beautiful machines, that we can make art and music that lasts long after we have been turned back into stardust. Thank you, Elon Musk, Douglas Adams, David Bowie.

We still have a lot of things to fix down here on earth, but if you gaze up for a moment, you'll know why human beings are compelled to do these things too. Because the stars look very different today.

Gooi it in the pot

Today I learned, or 'TIL', as they say on Reddit, that the Afrikaans word for podcast is 'potgooi'.

I smaak this coinage a lot, partly because it seems like a small act of defiance in the face of mass globalisation – a podcast is a podcast is a podcast in pretty much every other language in the world – but mostly because it is such an evocative and engaging term on its own merits.

When I think of potgooi, I picture people standing around a potjie, gooiing little titbits into the slow-brewing conversation. It has a casual, convivial, make-the-circle-bigger ring to it – you can almost smell the brandewyn swirling in the stew.

Podcast, on the other hand, is a lingering tribute to the power Apple wields in our social and cultural lives.

The word was minted in 2004 by a UK tech journalist, Ben Hammersley, as a portmanteau of 'iPod', Apple's breakthrough MP3 player, and 'broadcast'.

While the iPod no longer exists as a separate device, it was hugely influential as the forerunner of all the portable iDevices that have come to hold sway over the way we see, hear, touch, and understand the world.

Except of course in Afrikaans, where the pot is a bigger force than the pod, and where almal is welkom om te kuier en om te gooi.

The benevolent imperialism of the BBC

It was a special type of thrill, the other night, to see the BBC World Service logo, in all its stately white-on-red Gill Sansibility, commanding the spotlight on the stage of the Market Theatre in Johannesburg.

The occasion was a recording of an episode of *Arts Hour on Tour*, the global radio roadshow that sets out to take the pulse of the world's most creative cities.

The format is a lively panel discussion, hosted by the amiable Nikki Bedi, with audience participation and interludes of performance.

This Jozi edition touched on such topics as street art, cinema, cultural taboos, land claims, minibus taxis and inner-city architecture, and featured a very funny stand-up set from the laid-back Limpopoan, Tsitsi Chiumya, as well as two knockout songs by the 'Future Ghetto Punk' singer, Moonchild Sanelly.

In the foyer before the show, I seized the opportunity for a chat with Mary Hockaday, whose official title is Controller of BBC World Service, English.

Given that the BBC World Service is by far the largest international broadcaster in the world, reaching an average of almost 280-million people a week, in more than 40 languages, on radio, television, and online, this is a position, as the English might say, of a not entirely inconsequential nature.

Mary stands right in the frontline of the fast-changing world of news and media, while at the same time representing an institution that is steeped in eight-and-a-half decades of tradition and authority.

There is something about listening to the BBC World Service that is as comforting and familiar as holding your hands around a mug of hot tea, wherever you may be in your corner of a foreign field.

When I suggest to Mary that the service is in some way a benevolent form of British Imperialism, she laughs politely and corrects me: 'I certainly like to think that we're benevolent,' she says, 'but I like to think of us more in a way as a sort of gift to the world.'

Aside from concise and lucid news bulletins at the top of every hour, that gift is the gift of curiosity, wonder, and deep, abiding engagement that is the hallmark of the service's excellent radio documentaries.

On an amble around my neighbourhood last week, using the free BBC iPlayer Radio app, I tuned into a show on the 60th anniversary of skateboarding in California; another on the phenomenon of 'open secrets' in professional wrestling and religion; and a short clip about a team of professional tree-climbers in Washington, whose speciality is rescuing stuck domestic cats.

The variety of content on the service is ear-boggling, and it is hard to choose in tone between the earnest, the upbeat, the train-spottingly obsessive, and the cheerfully eccentric, so in the end one chooses a buffet sampling of them all.

I asked Mary whether there is such a thing as a typical BBC World Service listener, and she said, 'It's not a particular type of person or age or demographic; it's just about an attitude of mind. It's people who are curious about the world, who want to know what's going on, who want to understand and hear from people who can illuminate and connect and share stories.'

In the beginning, which was 1932, the BBC World Service was primarily intended as a light cast across the waters, to 'men and women, so cut off by the snow, the desert, or the sea, that only voices out of the air can reach them', as King George V put it in his Christmas message.

In her Controlling position, Mary is acutely aware of the heritage of the service, which culturally is still associated with the plumminess of Received Pronunciation – the accentless, perfectly articulated English of Broadcast House, where London, as The Clash reminds us, is forever calling.

But at the same time, the BBC, which is funded by the public rather than the state, has a cherished reputation for the accuracy and impartiality of its news, reported by correspondents in the furthest-flung places on the globe. 'And I don't want to mess with that at all,' says Mary.

What is changing and evolving is the diversity of voices, subjects, and digital and social platforms, all of which combine to produce a service that strives to be 'engaging, fresh, outward-looking, open-minded, and open-hearted'.

The news, the spine of the BBC World Service, says Mary, remains what it has always been: the stuff that is new and important in the world.

'But the news can sometimes feel like a rather relentless diet of the terrible things,' she concedes. 'We will continue to report those things, because nobody wants to shy away from reality. But we also, in the breadth of what we do, offer stories where we can show people engaging, trying to change things for the better, and making a difference across boundaries or divisions.'

Blood and heart: the day the Springboks came to town

The only Springbok garment I was able to find in my cupboard, at short notice, was a vintage model from the 2011 Rugby World Cup, the one the All Blacks narrowly won on home turf.

Still, it was green and it was gold, and there was the Bok pronking on the front, with the Faf-Speedo flag in pride of place on the bicep. So I slipped the T-shirt on – it fitted, loosely, I think because the whole range is tactfully designed to accommodate boeps of all shapes and sizes – and I ordered myself an Uber.

Muderwa in a Corolla arrived within three minutes, and when he saw my shirt, he said, above the music, that the Boks would have won even if they had lost, because they had played with such blood and heart.

He tapped his fist against his chest as he said this, the way the Boks do when they line up to sing the anthem. 'Blood and heart,' he said. 'That's what makes them strong.'

I got out on Juta Street, in the heart of artisanal-hipster Braamfontein, with Wits just up the road, and the Nelson Mandela Bridge, with its stately masts and riggings, leading the way into town.

In the chromium heat of a highveld summer day, the kind that holds the hope of lightning and rain in its circuitry, I could smell boerewors sizzling on the braai.

I followed my nose to Bertha Street, and there I saw three okes, standing around a double-cab Hilux, the wors gushing in a pool of fat on the Cadac.

They were wearing T-shirts just like mine, and were sipping Windhoeks and Castles from the bottle. The spiral horns of a kudu bull were affixed to the front of the bakkie, which itself was festooned with flags, so I surmised that they must have travelled a long route overland to get here.

But when I asked one of the okes where they had come from, he shrugged his beer and said, 'Ag, Parkhurst,' which is, like, 10 minutes up the road.

He folded a stuk of wors into a Portuguese roll, and looking around, he saw a stern-faced gogo wearing a Hands Off Venezuela T-shirt, with the hammer and sickle of the South African Communist Party rampant.

'Would you like one?' he said, offering her the boerie roll, and the gogo nodded and took it and sat regally on a canvas camping chair to wait for the parade.

Further up Jan Smuts, the crowd was spilling from the pavement onto the street, and the best efforts of the SAPS and the Metro Cops and the private security – Bad Boyz, complete with twirly wired earpieces, like agents of the Secret Service – could not keep them at bay.

The street was getting narrower and narrower, and every car and truck and bus and minibus taxi that squeezed into the gap was greeted with whistles and whoops and cardboard signs of welcome and swirls of flag, as if in rehearsal for the real thing.

In turn, they hooted, but everyone hoots in Joburg, so it was hard to tell if they were Bok supporters or just Joburg drivers.

A guy was wandering through the crowd, bearing a pad of green ink and a Bok-shaped stamp, and people instinctively shook their heads when he approached them, the Joburg sign for sorry, I haven't got anything on me.

But all he wanted to do, for free and mahala, was anoint them with the Sign of the Bok, on their arms or their hands or the side of their face.

I strolled back down to Bertha, anointed, and out of nowhere, four young guys, wearing flags as capes and flags as underpants – Springbroekies, I believe they're called – dashed whoopingly across the road, beneath a banner that read #BokBefok.

There were rumours that the bus was on its way, but they were like the rumours of the rain: it didn't, and instead there were cloudbursts of song, murmurs rolling into swells into full-throated choruses, 'Shosholoza' rolling into 'Nkosi Sikelel'' into 'Hier Kommie Bokke'.

And then you couldn't hear a word of song, because everyone was pointing, waving, jumping, surging forward to meet the bus.

In the squinting distance of the cross-street, it looked to me like a big green warship, making its way home from the Odyssey, the warriors silhouetted against the silvery clouds, the sun carving a beam of light from the golden chalice.

I looked up when the bus was right next to me – I could taste the choke of its diesel, the waves of heat shimmering off the chassis – and I saw the takkies of the Boks, dangling over the edge.

And then Siya Kolisi, the Captain, acknowledging the cheers of the crowd, put his fist to his chest and held out his arm, and I understood that gesture for the first time: I am of you, it means; we are blood.

Someone down below, holding a rugby ball, caught his eye, and Siya beckoned: 'Throw.' The ball arced up to the top of the double-decker, and Siya caught it and signed and passed it around.

The school blazers flew, the school ties, the T-shirts, like gifts to the gods, and the gods threw them back, inscribed.

I followed the bus, jostled like flotsam by the throng, across the Nelson Mandela Bridge, into town, stopping at FNB Bank City, past the City Hall and onto Simmonds, at the edge of the freeway to Soweto, and everywhere I saw a certain look on the faces in the crowd.

They were lost in the moment, unblinking, a light shining in their eyes, and I saw that look, finally, as something beyond joy, beyond pride, beyond, even, hope.

It was a sense of wonder, an exultation of the spirit, just a heartbeat away from love. And even though I didn't take a selfie, I had the feeling that I was wearing that look too, on the day the Springboks, the 2019 Rugby World Cup champions, came to town.

Living in the shadow of a fatwa

In the open courtyard of The Campus in Bryanston, Johannesburg, where smoking is permitted, Zineb El Rhazoui plucks a Vogue Slim from the carton, lights it up, and takes a long, deep draw.

She's just finished her presentation at the annual Oslo Freedom Forum, a 'Davos for Revolutionaries', as *The Guardian* calls it, and the relief on her face is palpable. It's not just that she was dying for a smoke; she was barely a minute into her talk before she said, her voice quaking: 'I can't get rid of the fear that someone from the audience will stand up and shoot me.'

Even now, in the cool Autumn twilight, a man in a suit comes up to her, taps her on the shoulder, and tells her he is on standby if she feels in any way under threat at any point during her stay. She smiles, nods her thanks, and flicks a head of ash into the tray.

Zineb lives in Paris, in the shadow of a fatwa, and by rough estimate, she has received more than 7000 death threats online. She has round-the-clock police protection in her home city: 'Even when I go to the supermarket to buy toilet-paper,' she says, 'I am surrounded by men in black.' And yet she does not seem fearful.

She burns with anger and defiance, driven by her belief that she has an inalienable right to do what she does, and what she does is speak and write her mind, freely. Zineb is a journalist, author, and commentator on public affairs. But more than that, and proudly so, she is an iconoclast.

Born in Casablanca, Morocco, she asked too many questions,

even as a schoolgirl, about the role of women in Islamic society, and what she felt was their subjugation under a traditionalist patriarchal regime.

She later co-founded a movement called MALI, the Alternative Movement for Individual Liberties, and was arrested three times, as a journalist, for her criticism of the government.

At the Sorbonne in Paris, she studied Arabic, English, and French, and one day, during the popular uprisings of the Arab Spring in 2011, the joint editors of a small satirical publication called *Charlie Hebdo* asked to interview her about her activities in the social and political struggles in her home nation.

They later offered her a job as a writer and columnist. She accepted. She specialised in writing about religious matters, in particular, Islam. In the first week of the new year in 2015, she was on a working holiday in Casablanca, mulling over whether she should jump on a plane and fly back to Paris for an editorial conference.

'But I felt lazy,' she recalls, 'so I just sent an email to the editor, to say what I wanted to write about that week. I was waiting for his office to tell me how many pages I had to fill.'

Instead, she received a call from another journalist, who said, where are you? Casablanca, she said, and he told her there had been shootings at the offices of *Charlie Hebdo* in Paris.

'In the beginning, I thought it could not be a big thing,' she says. 'I thought a mad guy came and shot and like, broke one or two windows.' But as she would later learn, there had been a massacre.

Twelve of her colleagues, including her editors, had been murdered, and 11 others wounded, by two gunmen, siblings aligned to Al-Qaeda. Zineb lights another cigarette.

For months after the attack, she says, she felt guilty about surviving. A psychologist told her the feeling was normal, a symptom of PTSD, and she later took her healing from it: 'I realised that actually, the only people who were guilty were the brothers, with their criminal ideology.'

In the aftermath of the massacre, when the death threats against her became 'very targeted' – she was the subject of two virulent hashtag campaigns calling for her head – friends told her to give up, find a safe haven, change her name. But to do that, she says, would destroy her anyway.

'The person who I am would not be existing anymore.' She is keenly aware, too, of the privileges she enjoys under the protection of the French state. Journalists in other countries, such as those investigating drug cartels in Mexico, have not been so lucky. 'I have a duty,' she says, 'to keep opening my big mouth.'

I ask Zineb whether there was ever any sense of restraint at *Charlie Hebdo*, any voice that cautioned against pushing the boundaries of satire and free expression too far. She shakes her head.

'None of us. None of us who were killed there or who are still alive, ever tried to pull back. As long as it's legal in France, as long as we respect the law, we considered it our duty to criticise all kinds of holy things, power, powerful people, religions.'

The French tradition of cartooning as a form of protest goes all the way back to the republicans who aimed their venomous quills at the church and the monarchy in the 19th century: 'When I make a cartoon about someone,' she says, 'it's not meant to please them.'

But even she draws a caveat, in a modern era where the notion of free speech routinely comes with terms and conditions attached.

'We can joke about anything as long as we do it with talent,' she says, 'as long as we do it with preserving the dignity of individuals. There is a big difference between criticising ideas and attacking people.'

In the land of liberté, égalité, et fraternité, she still sees herself as a revolutionary, and her ultimate cause, her big wish, is that the Women's Revolution will one day succeed.

'I don't know a single country where people can say, okay, women and men are definitely enjoying the same rights,' she says.

From across the lawn, a man approaches. He apologises for interrupting the conversation, and tells Zineb how powerful he found her presentation. Then he says, eyeing the pack, do you mind if I bum a cigarette?

She offers him a Vogue Slim, and sparks her lighter, and in that moment, the wisp of the flame looks like the most dangerous of all things, the flicker of a fragile idea that can set the world on fire.

The wolf who came in from the wild

Every *Canis domesticus* has a contract to fulfil, the genesis of which harks all the way back to that fateful night on the steppes of Siberia, when the wild wolves drew closer to the flickering fire.

Perhaps one of our kind flung a scrap of meat at the pack, to appease them or scare them away; perhaps a bolder, hungrier wolf surged forward and made off with the prize.

Either way, at that moment, the ancient barrier between the species was breached, and an accord was struck, an understanding born of symbiosis.

The wolf, or at least the domesticated sub-genus thereof, would watch over and protect us, while we in turn would provide sustenance and shelter.

Somewhere along the line, the unspoken contract expanded its parameters, and the bounds of fidelity, trust, and companionship were shifted to accommodate love.

Pinky came to us via Puppy Haven in Johannesburg, and at first she was a foster, spindly-legged and rickety, with a tail like an apostrophe and a mottled nose that was the source of her name.

The idea was that we would feed her as per strict instructions, get her used to a household environment for a few weeks, and then return her safely to her haven for adoption.

This I duly did, because that, after all, was our contract with Puppy Haven, but on the way back, my phone beeped with an urgent SMS from my son, Max: 'Dad, please can we keep Pinky!!!'

What could I do?

I made a U-turn, signed a new set of papers, and brought Pinky home. Over the years, she kept her side of the bargain with a vigilance that was high in volume and low in bite, woofing bristle-backed at every bzzzz of the buzzer, at every beep of a hooter at the gate, at every wayward cat that snuck over the wall. At our own cats, too, whenever they climbed a tree or onto the roof, at which point, according to some stringent hierarchy, they miraculously transformed from friendly fellow-creatures into aloof and brazen threats to her standing on the social ladder.

Pinky had an expansive barkabulary, and the more we tried to shhhh her, the louder she got, especially when the keys jingled and the car-door opened and the breeze that blew through the window carried the mingled scents of the open fields in its slipstream.

Yesterday, Pinky, after almost 11 years as our *Canis lupus familiaris*, went off in spirit to join her ancestors on the snow-covered Siberian steppes, or perhaps the searing desert plains of Africa. Who knows, really, where the lineage began, or how our species first got to know each other.

But anyone who has ever had a dog in the household will know that the bonds run deep and strong, and the memories live on. Because we live out our lives in dog-years, and dog-years, whether you are a dog or a dog's best friend, are the happiest years of them all.

The capital crime of using uppercase

O n the internet, as we all know, communicating with your caps-lock key on lockdown is a capital offence known as SHOUTING.

It is the quickest way to lose an argument, or start a new one, even if all you are doing is saying GOOD MORNING!!!, or asking if anyone knows how to fix a stuck caps-lock key.

There is something about the looming heft of UPPERCASE TYPE, all those pumped-up letters standing to attention like an army about to march over the hill, that is guaranteed to induce anxiety in sensitive souls.

It is thus not surprising, according to a report in *The Week*, that lecturers at Leeds University in the UK have been advised NOT to use capital letters when communicating with students, for fear of leaving them feeling frightened or demotivated.

Interestingly, these are JOURNALISM students we are talking about, and if ever there was a profession where people talk to each other in capital letters ALL THE TIME, it has to be journalism.

This is a lingering legacy of the era of hot-metal publishing, when you had to shout to make yourselves heard above the din of letters being hammered onto hissing sheets of metal that would then be transformed by some mysterious alchemy into the paper you hold in your hands.

'Hold the front page!' someone would yell from across the newsroom, and then someone would hold it and get the edges of their fingers burned, and would yell even louder in turn.

Nowadays, the journalistic production process is a lot quieter, consisting as it does chiefly of journalists stealthily copying and pasting tweets from Twitter.

Years ago, when I worked on the West Rand bureau of *The Star*, in a pokey little office in Krugersdorp, I used to send my stories through to Head Office using a technology known as teletype, or telex.

The vehicle for achieving this was an armour-plated device with a keyboard and a rotary dialler, a sort of a cross between a tank and a typewriter, that would dispatch text on a scrolling sheet of paper via the telephone network.

The racket it made while doing so, with the type-head zipping to and fro across the page, was akin to lava rocketing onto a corrugated-iron roof, and the singular quirk of this mode of communication was that the telex could type only in CAPITAL LETTERS.

Then, once received extremely loud and clear on the other side, it would be the job of someone else to cut the excess caps down to size, and herd them into ranks of discreetly whispering lowercase.

And yet, the tradition of the shouty teletype continues even today, in the form of the all-caps newspaper poster, the theory being that uppercase looks more important and urgent and worthy of your attention while you are driving down the freeway, SHOUTING to make yourself heard above the din of the news of the day.

Remembering the Radio Rats, the eternal hope of Springs

The Radio Rats occupy a special place in the pantheon of South African rock 'n roll. Actually, not so much the Pantheon, which was a temple in Ancient Rome, as the Palladium, which was a bioscope in Springs.

Every great musical movement has its wellspring, its epicentre, its point of gravity around which the whole world revolves.

In the case of The Beatles, it was Liverpool; Bruce Springsteen, New Jersey; Nirvana, Seattle; Detroit, pretty much everyone with Soul, plus Iggy Pop.

So why not a small mining town to the far east of Joburg? Springs, in the South African psyche, is almost a one-word joke, a synonym for the grimy edge of nowhere, and while the bubbling fountains that gave it its name are long gone, it is home to some of the loveliest Art Deco architecture in the world.

And let's not forget that the Nobel Prize-winning author, Nadine Gordimer, was born here too. So were the Radio Rats.

Their Dr Frankenstein was a young medical student named Jonathan Handley, who was good at poetry in school, and who had a knack for turning his poems into tight, pithy pop songs, lyrically witty and infused with a touch of glam.

In 1977, the year that punk exploded in London, Jonathan formed the band that became the Radio Rats, with the growly-voiced Dave Davies on vocals, David 'Herbie' Parkin on bass, and more temporary drummers than you can shake a couple of drumsticks at.

The story of the Radio Rats is the story of every band that ever jammed in a small town from which they hoped their music would set them free, and it is told now, in loving, gritty detail, in *Jiving and Dying*, a documentary by the Durban-based filmmaker Michael Cross.

The doccie kicks off with a needle on a groove, a quote from the philosopher Claude Lévi-Strauss, and the familiar strains of the one-hit-wonderful 'ZX Dan', a ditty about a spaceman who is seduced by the sounds of rock 'n roll and falls in love with an earthling who plays it on her radio.

Cross makes the genius decision to shoot in grainy black-and-white, to match his archival footage, and the result is a movie that feels mined as much as made, coated with the texture of silica and the toxic dust of the mine-dumps.

In between the interviews with the surviving pack of Rats, Cross weaves the broader story of Springs and the rock 'n roll movement that sprang from it, especially its patron saint, the multi-talented James Phillips, who became Bernoldus Niemand and sadly died in 1995, years before his time.

Like James, the Radio Rats never really made it big, but they made it, and that's what really counts.

I loved this movie, which is in turn raucously funny, revelatory, sweetly poignant, profound in its reflections on the meaning of music and mortality, self-conscious in a very South African way, and refreshingly self-deprecating.

'We never copied anyone else,' Jonathan tells the interviewer. 'Because we weren't that good, we played our own stuff, and then nobody knew whether it had been played badly or not.'

The only pity about *Jiving and Dying* is that it won't ever be screened in the Palladium in Springs, because the Palladium, sadly, doesn't exist anymore. But the pantheon of South African rock 'n roll certainly does, and within its walls, playing loudly enough to bring them tumbling down, the Radio Rats will forever jive on.

Ask not for whom the giant ships come and go

'A ship is safe in harbour, but that's not what ships are for.' Under heavy cloud, the *Zhong Xin Pearl*, a bulk vessel registered in Hong Kong, set course for Singapore from Durban Harbour one morning this week.

As I watched the leviathan gliding on the wavelets, the little pilot ship churning water at its stern, like a kid waving goodbye to a grandparent going off to war, I thought about a seminar I attended in Joburg a couple of years ago.

Malcolm Gladwell, the Canadian author and journalist, was talking about one of the great unsung innovators of the modern era, a man whose name is virtually unknown outside of the industry where he made his fortune: trucking and transport. His name was Malcolm McLean.

The most familiar mantra of innovation, much-parroted in boardrooms and business schools, is Think Outside the Box. Shatter the boundaries, redraw the frame, open your mind to infinite space.

But Malcolm McLean did exactly the opposite. Frustrated by the haphazardous storage of goods in moving vehicles, he designed a secure, stackable metal box that first took to the roads, and then the waters, in 1956.

Thus, in a dazzling stroke of inside-the-box thinking, was the age of containerisation born. With hindsight, every earth-changing, life-transforming, disruptive technology seems inevitable and obvious.

But the container proved to be an instant revolution, and the chain reaction ignited by its simplicity and ease of use has radically altered the workings of the global economy.

Entire docks, entire cities, entire oceangoing vessels, had to be reconfigured to accommodate the standardised containers – they're known as TEUs, or Twenty-foot Equivalent Units – that now transport goods and commodities across the globe. At any given point, there are some 20-million such containers on the water.

They bring us, as end-users, almost everything we wear, use, and consume, in whole or constituted form, from clothes to electronics to food to machinery to appliances to cars to the fuel that drives them.

In her fascinating book on the subject, *Ninety Percent of Everything*, the journalist Rose George writes that it is cheaper for Scottish cod to be shipped to China for filleting, and then sent back to Scotland for sale in shops and restaurants, than it is to have them filleted around the corner.

This is because mass-containerisation has brought about economies of scale that can be factored into the supply and distribution of every commodity worth producing, manufacturing, and selling.

We are what we are, we eat what we eat, we use what we use, because of the giant ships that come and go. And yet, how often do we spare them even a moment's thought, when we are not beside the seaside?

'How ironic,' writes Rose George, 'that the more ships have grown in size and consequence, the less space they take up in our imagination.'

If we do pay heed to them at all, it is most often in the negative: the oil tanker that spills its load, the super-vessel that is boarded by pirates on the high seas, the container that dispatches billions of little plastic nurdles to the shore.

But this week, at the end of a stroll on the beautiful new promenade on the southern strip of the beachfront in Durban, I stood for a while and looked out at the channel of water between the breakwater dolosse and the dark green loaf of the Bluff, and I thought to myself: ask not for whom the giant ships come and go. They come and go for thee.

Paul Simon, the kid who fell short of his greatest dream

I am reading: *Paul Simon: The Life*, by Robert Hilburn, an eye-opening and illuminating biography of one of the great singer-songwriters of the modern age.

An early revelation, for me, was that the young Simon, despite his father being a professional musician – a double-bass player and bandleader in a big jazz band – had only a fleeting interest in music, and showed no desire to pursue it as a hobby, a passion, or, heaven forbid, a career.

Instead, growing up in a middle-class neighbourhood in the borough of Queens in New York City, Simon was possessed by an obsessive, consuming devotion for the all-American pursuit of baseball.

He was a fanatic (the word 'fan' seems too flippant) of his home team, the New York Yankees, the winningest franchise in the Major League, whose roster of legends includes Babe Ruth, Lou Gehrig, Joe DiMaggio, Mickey Mantle, and Yogi Berra.

As a child, Paul Simon was such a Yankeephile that he insisted on wearing a Lone Ranger mask to hide his sense of betrayal when his dad took him to a ballgame at the home ground of his team's fiercest rivals, the Brooklyn Dodgers.

Naturally, Simon played baseball too, and he dreamed of one day wearing the distinctive blue-pinstriped uniform of his heroes.

He was a talented player, named in his high school's all-star team as a pitcher, and he once made the *Long Island Press* for his superb performance in one of the game's key manoeuvres: 'Simon Steals Home', read the headline.

It was only years later, when he got to college and tried out for the team, that he realised he had no chance of ever making it in the big league.

He was just too short to reach the heights, in a sport where many of the best players are six-footers and over. But another passion had already begun to weave its way into his life.

One day, as Simon sat down at home to listen to a broadcast of a Yankees game on WINS radio, his finger hovered over the dial as the announcer, on another station, introduced what he said was 'the worst record I've ever heard'. That was enough to catch his ear.

The song was 'Gee', by The Crows, a doo-wop outfit from Harlem. 'Ohh-ohh-ohh, gee-ee,' went the opening verse, to a popping, shuffling beat, and Simon was mesmerised. It was like nothing he had ever heard before. The giddy harmonies, the simple lyrics, the swooning aura of youthful infatuation. In that moment, his world spun into a different orbit.

As fate would have it, two blocks down, a new family had moved into the neighbourhood. The Garfunkels. They had a son by the name of Arthur, or Art.

The two boys became friends, united by their common love of baseball. In the sixth grade, they were cast in a school production of *Alice in Wonderland*, with Simon in the lead singing role of the White Rabbit, and Garfunkel in a non-singing role as the Cheshire Cat. That's how far I am in the book.

For now, at last I understand that line about Joe DiMaggio in Mrs Robinson, and also why, sometimes, the best thing that can happen to you in life is that you fall short of your one great dream, and land, in a moment of cosmic serendipity, in another.

Farewell, matric

Children are born in grace and light, whipped into being by atoms of stardust that swirl through space and time.

One moment, you're holding them in your arms, gazing down at this stranger who looks strangely like you, and their greeting to the world is a wail of liberation, a deep gasp of air that shakes the cosmos to its foundations.

The next moment, in the flicker of an eye, they're sitting in the backseat of your car, tapping away on their phone, fretting in a froth like the rabbit in *Alice in Wonderland*: 'We're going to be late! We're going to be late! Hurry, we're going to be late!'

This was just en route to the pre-party, after which came the dance, after which came the after-party, after which the sun rose on the new world beyond. Where do all the hours go, the moments, the years, when they rush by at such a dizzying speed?

The answer lies somewhere out there in the swirl of space and time. But on this night, in this frozen moment, the night of the big matric dance – the night she has been speaking and dreaming about pretty much since her first day of high school – here stands Rachel, shining as brightly as a star.

The quiet gift of music when the power goes out

Last night, just after sunset, a great curtain of cloud fell from the sky, and there was a whip-crack of lightning, and the power tripped. I'm used to this; it's a T & C of life on the Highveld.

I dashed outside as the first drops began to splatter, and I opened the mains box to flip the switch to the up position. But it was already up.

That could mean only one other thing, and it was swiftly confirmed by the stream of WhatsApps on the neighbourhood group.

There was a widespread power outage, stretching all the way from Sandton and across the northwestern suburbs. Someone said it had been caused by Eskom cutting trees to prevent them from falling on power lines during the storm. In the process, a tree had fallen on a power line, cutting off the supply in a shower of sparks.

Technicians had been dispatched, confirmed the City Power Twitter account. There was no ETA for restoration. Darkness cloaked the streets, and within, torchlight speared the way down the corridors.

The emergency load-shedding light, on the kitchen table, shone too brightly to look in the eye. From the house next door, the smug purr of a generator. We got out the Cadac, its blue-yellow whoosh signalling the backup plan for supper.

There comes a point, during a power outage, when you walk around the house and switch the lights off, because by the time they come back on, you would have switched them off anyway.

It was around 10 pm, after doing this, that I poured myself a cup of tea from the whistling camping-kettle, and I sat down to flick through Twitter on my phone, hoping to see if there was an update on the ETA. There wasn't.

Instead, a news item caught my eye. 'Mark Hollis, Talk Talk star, dies aged 64'. I sat there, in the hush – even the generator had gone to sleep – stunned, for a moment.

I pictured a star flickering in the night sky, and then disappearing. But the thing about musicians, is that they never fade away.

I tapped onto Spotify, and searched for *Spirit of Eden*. Sometimes, you hear an album that seems to have been made for an audience of one. You imagine that no one else has heard it, that it is a gift to you alone.

Over the years, you discover that there are many other people who think this way, for whom the music chimes a secret chord that resonates on a hidden wavelength.

In the mid-1980s, Talk Talk were a highly successful synth-pop trio, with a string of Top 40 singles in the UK and beyond.

Then, in 1986, they sequestered themselves in a studio that was once the hall of a church, St Augustine's in Highbury, and over the space of a year, with the only light coming from flickering candles and strobes, they recorded the album that would effectively end their career as a pop group.

The legend says that when executives at EMI first heard the finished album, it brought tears to their eyes, not because the music is beautiful – it is – but because, as they later claimed in a contractual-obligation suit that dragged on in court for months, it was 'not commercially satisfactory'.

There are no easy hooks on *Spirit of Eden*, no hummable melodies, no steel-hammered template of verse-verse-chorus-bridge-verse-chorus.

The music on the album is a cycle of six songs, brooding and meditative, with silences you can fall into, and an eccentric array of instruments, including oboe, blues harp, bassoon, harmonium, dobro and muted trumpet, that play their parts in interweaving curlicues of improvisation.

There is only one drum-break on the album, midway through the more than seven-minute long 'Desire', and it is one of the most ecstatic bursts of pure rhythm in the history of popular music.

The vocals by Mark Hollis are sleepy-eyed incantations that ache with yearning, and in hundreds of listens over more than 30 years, I don't think I've understood more than a couple of words; I've never looked them up on a lyric site, for fear of breaking the spell.

And yet, *Spirit of Eden* is a daring, mesmerising masterpiece, as radical in its own way as Stravinsky's *The Rite of Spring* or *Kind of Blue* by Miles Davis.

You can hear in these tracks the eerie pre-echo of Coldplay and Radiohead and all the other downbeat, introspective pop bands that would follow years later, but this is the original, the Rosetta Stone, and it seeps into your pores like no other music ever made.

I listened in the darkness, and the songs, and the silences in their spaces, shimmered with an incandescent glow, like the pulses of light you see when you close your eyes. Goodnight, Mark Hollis, star of Talk Talk, and thank you for the quiet storm of your music.

When art is a happy accident

'A happy accident,' explained Hermann Niebuhr, the Johannesburg artist, when I asked him about the provenance of a work called 'Prophet' at his latest exhibition at Hodgins House Art Studio and Gallery, 4 Loch Avenue, Parktown.

The exhibition is entitled 'Everything', and it consists of a selection of moody landscapes and a couple of cityscapes, with words or phrases floating in their midst like portents from the Book of Daniel.

A fire burning a scar on a blackened mountain, with SPIRIT emblazoned on the smoke-cloudy sky; a range of hillocks unfolding towards a threatening storm, with 'go inside' whispering in cursive script; a fiery sunset silhouetting a cluster of trees, with the injunction 'don't look away' breaking the darkness.

The paintings illuminate the words; the words contextualise the paintings. They tussle in paradox, conflict, and counterpoint, and when I wondered aloud about the Biblical allusions here – the word 'Prophet', and an ornately decorated book imposing its heft, like a watermark – Hermann offered a wry smile and a shrug: 'In the beginning,' he said, 'was the word.'

It turns out that Hermann first painted the book, which is in fact a medieval tome in Italian, and then decided, as artists often do, to paint over it, to consign it to a layer of distant memory. To begin again.

But then, as he began working on this exterior view of his studio in Fordsburg, the book refused to be forgotten: it shone through, like a sunburst of revelation after the flood. So he let it be.

A happy accident of epiphany and synchronicity, leaving the viewer with two works for the price of one.

My favourite painting in the exhibition is the other cityscape, of a streetlamp shining a pool of orange light on the shores of a dark street, and the word upon it is SACRED, which I first read as SCARED.

It made me think immediately of 'The Sound of Silence', with its evocation of the words of the prophet, the writing on the wall, and the halo of the streetlamp.

And then, in turn, I thought of a tale of the creation of a song, recounted in *Paul Simon: The Life*, by Robert Hilburn. When Simon was composing what would prove to be his magnum opus, 'Bridge Over Troubled Water', one of the greatest gospel songs of all time, with its resonant theme of comfort in a time of need, he was stuck for a crescendo, a line of dramatic uplift that would lead the melody towards the heavens.

He just couldn't figure it out, until, one morning, watching his wife at the time, Peggy Harper, despairing over her greying locks in the mirror, he offered her an affectionate note of reassurance. He called her: 'Silver girl'.

And that became the line that became the verse. 'Sail on silver girl, Sail on by, Your time has come to shine, All your dreams are on their way'.

Likewise, many years later, Simon was leaving a dinner party in Manhattan when a fellow guest, in a perfectly understandable moment of nomenclative befuddlement, addressed the world-famous singer as 'Al'.

And that became the bass-popping, brass-blaring hit song on the *Graceland* album, 'You Can Call Me Al'.

Thus are paintings and songs born, in moments of cosmic insight and unintentioned awakening, to become the happy accidents of art that enlighten and enliven our world.

The curious South Africanisation of Black Friday

I had an hour to mooch between meetings today, so I mooched around Rosebank Mall. I wasn't alone. That's because today, as you may have noticed, was Black Friday, the fourth Friday in November, a day previously known on the South African calendar simply as 'Friday'.

But in the new global economy, where ideas and information flow like the waters of the ocean, it shouldn't be too surprising that the rituals and traditions of American retail should splash over onto our shores.

We don't observe Independence Day on 4 July; we don't observe Thanksgiving; we don't observe Halloween – oh, wait we do – and now, we observe Black Friday too.

The peculiar thing about this particular retail holy day is that it has no social, cultural, religious or historical context or connotation whatsoever. Its sole reason for being is to persuade consumers to buy stuff, an existential impulse that imbues the day with a raw honesty that other such occasions lack.

There are no hearts on Black Friday, no bunnies, no tinsel, no spooky *Scream* masks. All I saw at the mall were bouquets of black balloons with 'Black Friday' printed on them, a clear indication that the window dressers and merchandisers had given up and gone home. What can one say about a day named Black Friday?

Well, I, for one, can say that I think it is a good and useful idea. Consumer confidence, a key measure of a nation's well-being, has been dropping in South Africa over the years, and even the big merchants, such as Massmart, Woolworths, Mr Price, Edcon, and The

Foschini Group, have been battling in the face of an overall decline in spending. For smaller merchants, especially those who have to grapple with the soaring cost of rental in malls, it's tougher still.

Thus, any topical themed event that gets consumers flocking to the stores, queuing up at midnight, charging down the aisles like the warriors in *Braveheart*, must surely, in the greater analysis, be a Good Thing. (I hasten to add that I didn't see any actual fighting at the mall. Everyone was very well behaved.)

Of course, we all know the psychology of the 'loss leader', whereby the customer is lured into the store by the promise of substantial discounts on certain items, in the hope that they will stick around to buy additional items at the full price.

We have all heard the argument, too, that Black Friday encourages people to spend more than they can afford on stuff they don't really need. But this happens every day of the year, not just Black Friday. It is the very foundation of commerce in a free-market society: advertising, marketing, promotion.

It is all very well to have an ideological aversion to rampant consumerism, but short of retreating into the woods, like Henry David Thoreau did in *Walden* – 'I went to the woods because I wished to live deliberately, to front only the essential facts of life' – how does one resist? We are all consumers.

We consume the essentials of survival; we consume the little luxuries and indulgences; we consume the Big Luxuries; we consume data and airtime; we spend, spend, spend.

What we spend our money on is a lifestyle choice, an individual choice, and we try to spend it, as much as we can, within the constraints of prudence and fiscal discipline. But nobody spends in a vacuum.

Every transaction, small or big, fuels the engine of the economy. The greater the consumer demand, the more items must be produced, the more factories must be built, the more jobs must be created; the more consumers must emerge, the greater the consumer demand.

This is the chain of value that binds us all, whether we choose to go the mall, whether we choose to spend or save, whether we only ever buy what we need or occasionally buy what we want.

Me, for the most part, I managed to resist. I do hope somebody else picked up that iPad Pro that I held in my hands, mulled over, and decided, even at R 3000 off on the Black Friday special, to stick around and wait for until the Boxing Day sale.

The oys and joys of
Tali's Wedding Diary

I finally got around to watching *Tali's Wedding Diary*, the South African mockumentary series now screaming on Showmax.

I say screaming, because Julia Anastasopoulos, who plays the titular Tali, so perfectly nails – as in nails skritching down a blackboard – the voice, accent, mannerisms, persona and neuroses of the northern suburbs Joburg kugel, freshly transplanted to the rarefied bubble of the Cape Atlantic Seaboard.

In real life, Anastasopoulos is a talented graphic artist (you may have seen her charming line-drawing murals at the MyCiTi central terminus in Cape Town, and the children's section of The Book Lounge in the city) who is best known for her YouTube series, *SuzelleDIY*.

But whereas Suzelle is all koeksister-sweetness and light, with her skyscraper beehive and her 1960s Pretoria Civil Service frocks, Tali is her bipolar opposite in every which way.

Her fine-spun hair betrays her gold-digging Joburg roots, and her midriff tops and designer jeans are cat-scratched in exactly the right places.

She speaks in a grating collision of diamond-hard consonants and elongated vowels, and she flutters her lashes just a fraction of a second too long, the better to let us catch the glitzy iridescence of her eye-shadow.

She is bitter, brittle, brash, conniving, spoiled, mean, entitled, selfie-obsessed, and so vain, Carly Simon could have written a song about her.

But somehow, wonder of wonders, miracle of miracles, Anastasopoulos ultimately makes Tali a likeable and empathetic character, by exposing her vulnerabilities and drilling down to the heart of taiglach that beats beneath that shallow exterior. (A taiglach is a confection of knotted fried dough, drooled with honeyed syrup, the Jewish cultural equivalent of a koeksister.)

The conceit of the eight-episode series is that Tali Shapiro has commissioned a video diary of the frantic run-up to her nuptials with fellow ex-Joburger Darren Nudelman, a close-cropped schlemiel (played with a moody, wistful intensity by Anton Taylor) who is trying, maybe too hard, to make it big in the inner-city property-gentrification game.

One of the joys and oys of *Tali's Wedding Diary* is that it makes no excuses or apologies for the narrowness of its context, the niche within a niche of a subset of Jewish Cape Town.

The viewer is left to figure out for themselves the broader context, the deeper subtext, and the precise meaning (even I had to google, I confess) of Yiddishisms like 'rachmonos', which are casually sprinkled into the naturalistic dialogue by Anastasopoulos and her co-writers, Ari Kruger and Daniel Shea Zimbler.

The result is a mockumentary that mirrors rather than mocks its characters, and much of my frequent laughter was the laughter of recognition – I know these people.

Even the easiest of targets, a bunch of Cape Town hippies holding a hey-shoo-wow party in a sub-plot, is played with a realness that makes them warm and relatable, and all the funnier for it. But let's delve into the subtext for a moment.

If *Tali's Wedding Diary* has a theme, beyond the wedding and the diary, it is Tali's total obliviousness to the real world and the real needs and emotions of the people in orbit around her.

As one gently exasperated character tells her, she needs to learn to 'stand outside herself', a revelation that cuts her to the core. In one of the funniest scenes, Tali commandeers a hotel boardroom for a PowerPoint presentation to her bridesmaids-to-be.

As the screen slowly descends from its moorings, it obscures Tali's poor, harassed, clipboard-clutching intern, Ashley, who just stands there and disappears. In the glare of Tali's ego, she becomes invisible. So does much of Cape Town itself.

We see Tali zooming around in her white Bee-Em with the sunroof and the vanity plates – TALIBBZ GP – scouting for a 'homeless person' to guilt-gift the leftover food in the polystyrene container alongside her. Eventually she finds one, swiftly winds down her window, and hands over the prize.

'It's teriyaki salmon!' she yells in her rear-view, as she speeds off towards her cocoon – her parents' spare luxury apartment in Bantry Bay.

In scenes like this, *Tali's Wedding Diary* chisels its politics between the lines, with a subtlety and sharpness that are rare in South African comedy. What are we to make, for instance, of the choice of date for Tali and Darren's Big Day – Human Rights Day, 21 March? None of the characters makes a comment about this, which is commentary enough on its own.

All of this makes the series enjoyable as a raucous, pacy farce of modern manners, or as a thought-provoking slice of life inside the bubble.

Either way, *Tali's Wedding Diary* is a landmark of South African television, and it marks the emergence, as a butterfly from a cocoon, of Julia Anastasopoulos as a major creative force.

She is supported by a sterling cast of characters, my favourites of whom were Rael Rosen, the up-and-hustling young wannabe property dev, whose mantra, re a sprawling warehouse in Salt River, is 'buy when there's blood in the streets'; and Andy, the jaundiced, cloth-capped ad agency 'creative', who takes on the thankless task of realising Tali's vision for her wedding, and who exacts his vengeance in an hilarious logo-based sight gag.

If you're not a Showmax subscriber, don't worry: you can sign up for a two-week trial and binge all eight episodes totally for free.

A fragment of history from behind the Grassy Knoll

This is a fragment of history, a splinter of a moment that changed the world, in a burst of rifle-fire on a Friday afternoon in Dallas, Texas.

I used to think, because I had read all the right books – or maybe they were the wrong books, looking back – that the final gunshot, the gunshot of the apocalypse, had come from somewhere up on the Grassy Knoll, where a sniper had been standing in wait behind the wooden stockade fence.

History itself is a coalition of fragments, a cluster of suppositions and probabilities surrounding a nuclear core of truth. The more you chip away at it, the more you try to worry the truth to light, the more you are left with splinters and dust in your hand.

The Assassination of the 35th President of the United States, John Fitzgerald Kennedy, has its own mythology, its own cast of characters, its own happy-never-after ending, and the only way to understand it, if not to solve it, is to go to the place where it happened and walk around for a while.

We were on honeymoon, many years later, travelling across the American South in a rented car: Charleston, Orlando, Memphis, New Orleans, Dallas. It was a quiet, sunny day when we stopped at Dealey Plaza on Elm Street.

I stood on the bright green grass in front of the white pergola, the sun-slatted walkway curled like an enfolding arm. When something terrible or important happens in a place, history gives the architecture a fresh coat of meaning, and the buildings will never quite look the same. They live and breathe; they have borne witness.

Sometimes, the buildings are torn down, because they have seen too much. But in Dealey Plaza, like time itself, they stand still.

I could hear the echo, the rush in my ears, the psychic pulse of the aftershock, as I stood on the concrete pedestal where Abraham Zapruder stood, shooting his home movie.

In my mind's eye, the flickering images seared into memory, I followed the sweep of the motorcade as it turned the corner, and disappeared for a moment behind the freeway sign, and emerged again into the sharp glare of day.

I walked a little further up the knoll, into the dappled shadows where the stockade fence stood, its pickets sharpened like spears.

I stood there, imagining what the sniper may have seen, if there had been a sniper. I watched a car go by, towards the triple underpass.

And then, as I touched the stockade, to test its texture, a sliver of it broke off and fell to the ground, like sand crumbling on the shore. I picked it up and stuck it in my pocket and walked away, towards the big brownstone box of the Texas School Book Depository.

Today the building is known as the Sixth Floor, because the southeast window of the sixth floor is where Lee Harvey Oswald stood and watched and waited with his rifle, his 6.5 mm Carcano Model 91/38 carbine, for the Presidential motorcade to pass below, just before half-past noon on Friday, 22 November 1963. Or so history tells us, if history knows the truth.

The Sixth Floor is now a museum, hushed and reverential, devoted to the life and times of John Fitzgerald Kennedy, and particularly to his last day in Dallas.

I wandered around the exhibits, and then I walked over to the southeast window, where a pile of cardboard boxes stood, sealed with masking-tape. The sniper's nest.

There is a pane of safety glass that stops you from going too far, but you can look beyond it, to see what Oswald would have seen, and when I did, my heart stopped for a moment.

I followed the path of a car on Elm Street, six stories below, and it seemed to be travelling in slow-motion, and I saw for the first time that this would have been the easiest shot, the easiest three shots in the world.

The assassin had the perfect lair, and he would have had the perfect moment. All he needed to do was look through the telescopic sight and pull the trigger, three times in six to eight seconds.

There was no need for anyone else, no need for a sniper on the Grassy Knoll. Oswald, alone, on the Sixth Floor. It felt like the truth, and it hit me with a jolt.

But still I have the fragment of wood from the picket fence, my souvenir of Dallas. And when I pick it up and turn it to the light, it sheds a few specks and leaves an imprint, a shadow on the white paper, like the Shroud of Turin, or the dust from a butterfly's wings.

A homeless Jesus

I was startled this icy morning, on my way to Wits University, as I wrapped my jacket closer against the chill, to see this figure huddled beneath a blanket on a bench.

I stopped in my tracks, my attention drawn by the hooded face-lessness of the figure, lying prone beneath the heavy folds of the blanket.

It took me a good couple of seconds to reassure myself that this is a statue, a bronze, as I learned called *Homeless Jesus*, by the Canadian sculptor Timothy Schmalz.

It is one of more than 100 placed on the fringes of churches around the world, including St Peter's Basilica in the Vatican, St Ann's Church in Manchester, England, and St George's Tron Church in Nelson Mandela Place in Glasgow, Scotland.

This *Homeless Jesus* lies outside the Holy Trinity Church that adjoins the Wits campus in Braamfontein.

It is one of the most powerful pieces of public art I have ever seen, a symbol of faith that is at the same time a symbol of our secular society, a reminder of just how easy it is to walk on by when we see a real person, homeless and alone, on the streets of a city built from gold.

Dining à la Eskom

Power outage in the neighbourhood. Again. In fact, we seem to have as many power outages as power innages these days. And even worse, these nights.

When the power goes out in Joburg, two things tend to happen. Firstly, Joburgers drive like Joburgers, just a little worse, because the robots aren't working.

Secondly, every restaurant and fast food joint that is lucky enough to have a generator does a roaring trade.

Tonight, I thought I would try a tiny fish 'n chip joint in Darrenwood, near Cresta Mall. It's called Fish Hook, and it prides itself on serving fish 'n chips in the authentic British style, which begins with having to stand in an authentically British queue.

The place was crowded. The battered-looking proprietor, battling to cope, asked if I would mind waiting 30 minutes for my order, which was Medium Fish 'n Chips, the other options being Small Fish 'n Chips and Large Fish 'n Chips.

Well, there isn't much else to do when you're out and about and the power is out, so I waited, soaking up the vinegary waft and the sh-sh-shake of the salt tin from the kitchen.

Forty minutes later, I had my fish 'n chips, which of course I dined on straight from the newsprint wrapping. (Thank goodness for fish 'n chip shops, without which the newsprint industry would be in really big trouble).

I have Mancunian roots; my grandfather on my mother's side ran a fish 'n chip shop in Roodepoort, west of Joburg – so I can safely say I know my fish 'n chips.

And these, even though I couldn't see them very well, were

among the best I've had in South Africa, at least on a par with those you get from that little joint in Kalk Bay, just without the seagulls to swoop down and peck them from your hands.

The real test of good, greasy, fresh-fried, thick-cut, newsprint-wrapped fish 'n chips is whether you feel a fleeting pang of guilt straight after scoffing them, because let's face it, they're not exactly the Real Meal Revolution. And boy, do I feel fleetingly guilty.

Even better than that, amazingly, the power has just this instant come back on. Thank you! In both cases, that was well worth the wait.

Mokgadi, the One Who Guides

he thing about being an athlete, that sets the athlete apart from the rest of us, is that athletes know, to the merest whittling of a second, exactly how good they are at what they do.

Their self-esteem is objectively quantifiable, calibrated according to the ever-adjusting currency of the PB: the Personal Best.

In the case of Mokgadi Caster Semenya, the reigning world champion in the women's 800 metres, that measure is: 1 minute, 54.25 seconds.

That makes her the fourth-fastest woman over that distance in history, separated from the Number One by less than a second, the crack of a pistol, an intake of breath, a whisper on the wind.

When I first catch sight of Caster in the lobby of 1 Discovery Place in Sandton, the thing that strikes me is the leonine grace of her walk, the way it conserves her energy at the same time as it stamps a regal aura on her surroundings.

For a moment, it seems odd – is this really Caster? – but then I realise it's because we are so used to seeing her on the sprint, ahead of the pack, her arms and legs a blur, and a few blinks later, standing in her victory pose, biceps flexed, hands pointed sideways. The pose of the Cobra.

The ritual of the race dictates that this must be followed by a crossing of the arms, a hug of self-celebration, at the apex of which her fingers whisk the imaginary stardust from her shoulders.

It is a gesture of pride, deflection, and untouchability that seems quite at odds with the gracious and reserved figure sitting across from me in the Wellness Centre, her Nike Flyknits – she is a Nike ambassador as well the ambassador of Discovery Vitality – glowing with the electric blue luminosity of a lightning bolt.

I ask Caster how, when you are the best in the world at something, it is possible to retain your humility, assuming that is even a good and necessary thing for an athlete to do.

She smiles a shy smile, and she draws a finger along the vein on her forearm. 'It's simple,' she says. 'I am just like you. I am human. I breathe the same air, I bleed the same blood. When I walk down the street, I am Caster Semenya. When I step onto the track, I am an athlete. When I win, I am a champion. Then it's done, and I walk out, and I am Caster again. It's like wearing a mask.'

Her voice is a deep and earthy drawl, the octave of thunder rolling on the horizon. Her first name, Mokgadi, is Sepedi for the One Who Guides, and that has been her destiny, her calling, ever since, as a little girl in the village of Fairlie, Limpopo, she began running for her life, first as a defender on the football field, then as a home-run hitter on the baseball diamond, then as a middle-distance runner on the athletics track.

I ask Caster whether she listens to music before she runs – what athlete doesn't? – and whether she has a favourite track, a song that guides her. She thinks hard about it for a moment. 'There are a lot of inspirational songs.'

Then it springs to mind: 'There is one in particular. It's about slaves, no slaves … something like that. I can't think of the title now. I'll find out and I will send it to you.'

Ah, is it 'New Slaves', by Kanye West, I offer, jumping the gun. 'No no no, not Kanye,' she shakes her head, and that makes her remember. It's a gospel song, called 'No Longer Slaves'. I listen to it later, at home.

'You unravel me, with a melody,' runs the opening lyric. 'You surround me with a song, Of deliverance from my enemies, Till all my fears are gone. I'm no longer a slave to fear, I am a child of God.'

The best of us, it turns out, are just like the rest of us. They fear less, they run faster. But they keep on running, over and over, again and again, because no matter how good they may be, they are driven to be better than their Personal Best.

A BlackBerry rings a bell

I chanced upon this picture while searching for a particular image in my Google
Photos library just now.

I don't recall taking it, but it dates from
2011, according to the info button, and the location is a shop in
the Cresta Mall.

Notices like this always stop me in my tracks, especially if they
are signed 'Management', because one of the perks of being a
manager is that you can order people around even if they don't
specifically work for you.

I also like the ambiguity at work here – is one allowed to touch
some of these cellphones, if not all? Or is the injunction merely
against touching all of the cellphones at once?

In any case, looking back now, it is amazing to see how cellphones have homogenised since the advent of the iPhone.

All phones are now, to some extent or other, glossy black slabs
without buttons on their face. Their design genesis is the mysterious black obelisk, an artefact of alien intelligence, that appears on
the surface of the moon in *2001: A Space Odyssey*.

I miss the BlackBerry, a model of which can be seen peeking
centrally beneath the sheet of paper here.

The BB had a physicality, a tactility, that made it very pleasur-
able to use – the keyboard was much more conducive to accuracy
and speed than any touchscreen keyboard I've ever used, and the
little red light that winked at you to let you know you had a message was pulse-quickening in a very Pavlovian way.

But eventually my BB, like all the others, gave up winking and any other kind of action, and it now lies forlornly in a drawer, a relic of the early Jurassic era of cellphone design.

The company itself, once the mightiest force in mobile, has all but disappeared, as has the once even-mightier Nokia.

We are all iPhoneys or Fandroids nowadays, and we all, all the time, touch all our cellphones.

I've completely forgotten what photograph I was looking for now, but I'm sure it will ring a bell eventually.

Bias, a street-art archaeologist of the future

In an alleyway in Braamfontein today, just off De Beer Street in the neighbour-hood of Neighbourgoods, the click-clack and hiss of aerosol spray-cans heralded an event of great signifi-cance in the street-art community of Johannesburg – the first Meeting of Styles South Africa, or MOS, to be held on the African continent.

MOS is an international network of graffiti artists and afi-cionados that hosts collaborative, sponsored 'graffiti jams' and exhibitions in cities around the world. This weekend was Joburg's turn.

I took a wander down the alley and saw some fascinating pieces taking shape, from faint early outlines into bright, textured showcases of contemporary urban art. A vibrant street art scene is critical to the cultural and social well-being of a modern, free-thinking city, and it's good to see Joburg leading the way.

This here is Bias, one of the city's most ubiquitous street artists, hard at work on a 3D abstract that incorporates, in signature style, his signature: the artist and his artwork, fused into one.

It's mesmerising to watch an artist at work, any artist, but a street artist in particular, because their works so often seem to appear from out of nowhere, brightening up and adding new meaning to drab and over-familiar landscapes.

And then, just as suddenly, the works seem to disappear, victims of the elements, inner-city 'clean-up' campaigns, or the falling of walls as a harbinger of redevelopment.

Street art is thus by its very nature ephemeral and transient, which is a big part of its allure and appeal: it shifts and mutates in line with the city itself. I waited until Bias had a few moments to chat, and then I grabbed a takeaway cappuccino and a flat white from Father Coffee around the corner, and we chatted.

I told Bias that this work-in-progress spoke to me of the dynamic bustle and energy of Joburg, in part because I saw a freeway and a freeway strut in it, and he smiled and told me it was going to turn out to be a spaceship. So I was almost right.

Bias is an archaeologist by profession, a candidate for a Phd, and he also works as street-art guide for the inner-city tourism company Past Experiences, one of the sponsors of this Meeting of Styles.

I asked Bias whether he saw any particular connection between archaeology and street art, and of course he did: 'I always say, with graffiti, you're adding layers to produce the future,' he said, 'and with archaeology, you're taking away layers to understand the past.'

Bias works with a quiet intensity, earphones plugged into his ears, and I was curious to know what he had been listening to while painting, because in my experience, artists and designers tend to have excellent taste in music.

'Oh,' he said, 'I usually listen to podcasts.' What kind of podcasts? 'Crime podcasts.' This led naturally to a brief sidebar on the perils of working in the great wide open in Joburg, and Bias nodded earnestly and said, 'I'm always very careful. But it's not crime that I'm worried about. It's mainly flash floods.'

This because much of the work that Bias produces is hidden from the public glare, in drainage tunnels, under freeway bridges, on the dim and barren edges of the city's infrastructure.

All art is in some way an expression and act of ego, but Bias describes himself as 'on the cusp between extrovert and introvert … I like being out there, but sometimes I need to calm down and find a quiet space, all to myself.'

And yet, even when they toil in the unseen spaces, graffiti artists and writers are benefactors of the public good: their work adds light and shade, commentary and context to the urban landscape, and on the walls of their inside-out galleries, they give us pause to stop and think and maybe understand our cities, as if for the first time.

Barry Hilton and the science of funny

Yesterday, just for laughs, I attended a workshop called 'Talk Funny', run by the well-liked entertainer and funny-talker, Barry Hilton.

Barry is one of the few clean comedians on the SA stand-up circuit, which is odd when you consider that he lives in Cape Town and hasn't had a bath in months.

There were a dozen of us at the workshop, ranging from a lawyer to a psychologist to a radio producer to the sports broadcaster and conference speaker, Arnold Geerdts, who is known for his sharp and easygoing wit at the podium.

Barry, who has the kind of elastic, panda-eyed face that is just perfect for a career in comedy, kicked off by asking us to estimate how many jokes he has told in more than 35 years of professional joke-telling.

Thousands of jokes? Millions of jokes? Several dozen hundred jokes? Then came the punchline. 'I've told three jokes,' said Barry, and he lowered his jaw and checked us out with his Barry Hilton face.

Of course there was a catch, and the catch was that there are only three types of jokes that Barry tells, woven into his shtick of physical comedy and observational humour.

There is the False Logic joke, an example of which is: 'Two fish in a tank. The one says to the other, you drive, I'll man the guns.'

The second type is the Exaggeration joke. Example: 'I used to be so overweight, I was a reserve for the whales in Hermanus.' And finally, the Pun.

Barry gave a real-life example, based on his appearance a few years ago in a court case over the, ahem, disputed ownership of a painting. 'Your Honour,' Barry told the magistrate, 'I've been framed.'

Three jokes, and within their orbit, an infinite variety. 'Let me explain it to you this way,' said Barry. 'What do you need to bake a loaf of bread?'

Happily, someone had the answer, which was: wheat, flour, and water. And how do you make olive bread? You add olives. And a cheese-loaf? You add cheese.

So to make jokes, if I understand Barry correctly, you just add olives and cheese. Then it was our turn to write a few jokes. 'Don't worry how kak they are,' said Barry, by way of encouragement.

We toiled for a while, using Barry's Einsteinian formula of 'A plus B plus C = Funny', and I came up with one about the water crisis in Cape Town, since I had just come back from a few days in Cape Town. Well, that's my excuse.

I took a deep breath and delivered my joke to the room. 'Did you hear about the new alphabet they're using in Cape Town?' I enquired. 'A B C D E F G, P Q R S T U V, W X Y and Z.' I paused for a moment. 'It's because they haven't got H2O.'

My apologies to Capetonians and everybody else, and my thanks to Barry Hilton, my Cousin and yours, for a highly entertaining and informative day of serious endeavour.

Stripping Gatsby bare

It is often said that we forget the names of the fleetingly famous, the mighty and the powerful who hold sway over our lives. But we never forget the names of our teachers.

I remember Miss Ramsay, who painstakingly took hold of my hand as I took hold of a pencil on the first day of Grade 1, showing me the correct way to draw the number 2.

I remember Miss Price, who read aloud my essay on going to feed the ducks at Florida Lake, as I squirmed with a mixture of pride and embarrassment at the back of the class.

I remember Miss Fraser, who made history come alive, and who spent at least half of every lesson telling us about her cats, and why they were infinitely superior to every human in history.

I remember my father, a teacher too, who would work until late at night in the holidays, marking papers and preparing the forthcoming curriculum.

And I remember Mr Cawdry. He was my English teacher in Standard 9. He was strict but fair, rigorous in his coverage of the syllabus but open-minded in his interpretation.

Our setwork for the year was *The Great Gatsby*, by F Scott Fitzgerald. Mr Cawdry handed out our paperbacks, and we very quickly noticed the black censor strips on the painting on the cover, mandated by the Education Department to save our young minds from being forever corrupted by this vision of 1920s decadence.

Then Mr Cawdry said, 'Before we begin reading, there's

something I need you all to do.' And he showed us how to scratch off the censor strips, bit by painstaking bit, until there was nothing but the naked and original artwork underneath.

Thank you, Mr Cawdry. Even if, I must confess, I'm still not 100 per cent sure what the green light at the end of Daisy's dock is supposed to symbolise.

Long live the academy

A graduation ceremony makes a university campus feel like the concourse of an airport, in the sense that it bustles with the energy of journeys coming to an end, and new journeys beginning in their place.

To graduate is to arrive, to have climbed a step, in the original Latin meaning of the word, but it is also to embark, to set off on the next adventure, the next stage of learning and becoming.

And in between, in a swirling moment of reflection, affirmation, and celebration, there is the ceremony.

This week was Graduation Week at Wits University, and the plaza in front of the Great Hall was thronged with graduandi and their guests, milling around in the weak Winter sunshine beneath a diamond-blue Johannesburg sky.

The strict classical geometry of the paving stones, and the perfect pleats of the Corinthian columns that heft the pediment of the façade, was complemented by the free-flowing swirls and patterns of fabric from across the continent: Shweshwe, Ankara, Kente cloth, Basotho blankets.

And then the gowns, draped like sails unfurled, their inky blackness accentuated here and there by sashes of dark blue or scarlet, harking back to a tradition nine centuries old, when the fellows of Oxford and Cambridge dressed according to the dictates of the clergy.

In the modern age, weaving together these threads of Grecian philosophy, medieval ritual, and African style, one accessorises. A pair of delicately tottering stiletto heels; a springbok-hide head-band; a necklace of beads; a hat with a brim wide enough to block out the sun.

On the steps of the Great Hall – so many steps, so many gradu-ates who have climbed them, over so many years – two gowned individuals wear the outsized heads of the kudu, an antelope famed for being the official emblem of Wits.

Mr and Ms Kudos Kudu, as they are known on campus, pose for selfies and group portraits, and then, precisely on schedule, comes the announcement for the entire herd of us to file into the auditorium.

Eventually we settle down, the hubbub of conversation filtering to a murmur, punctuated by the flip-flapping of the pages of the glossy programme, which commands: 'The audience will rise as the academic procession enters the hall, and will remain standing until the Chancellor is in place.' We rise.

The academics file in, the bright colour of their gowns flagging their status, their pace swift and sure, their faces mostly stern, with a hint now and then of a wry or gentle smile.

The Chancellor, Justice Dikgang Moseneke, is in place, behind the wooden podium, with the ceremonial mace in front of him, his scarlet gown flanked with threads of black and gold, a tassel dan-gling jauntily from the soft Tudor bonnet on his head.

'Gaudeamus igitur,' sings the Wits University choir, standing on the stage, 'Juvenes dum sumus.' That lusty, jocular song of rejoic-ing, of pleasant youth and troublesome dotage, of the memories of those who have gone before us, the students and the professors, who have long crossed over into the celestial realm or the inferno below, of the eternal triumph of the academy over the devil.

'Quivis antiburschius, atque irrisores.' Let whoever is against our school, who laughs at it, perish! The final notes fade away, a pause for breath, and straight into 'Nkosi sikelel' iAfrika'. We are seated, and the Chancellor constitutes the congregation.

'Never let it be said that any of us lack the agency to work hard,' he says. He has just returned from a visit to Russia, and he tells the story of a church in Moscow that took 65 years to build. Faith takes time, faith in the self even more so.

'Believe in yourself, in your greatness, and never, ever be afraid to shine,' he says. It is time for the graduates to shine. I count their number in the programme: 312 in total, across the faculties of Engineering and the Built Environment, Humanities, and Science.

One by one, their names are called, and they walk up, from stage-left to stage-right, a steady procession of smiles and nods and handshakes, the handing over of scrolls, the doffing of heads, the conferring of sashes by the Acting President of Convocation, who stands on a small platform so that he is better able to confer.

The song that the choir will sing is 'Ihele': 'Here is a procession, a procession of our champions, a procession of people of knowledge, a procession of our heroes.'

Everyone who has come to see the ceremony has come to see the champions, the heroes, the people of knowledge, but everyone, too, has come to see one in particular: their own.

The hall reverberates with shouts of 'halala!' and bursts of applause as each name is called, and we are on page 16 of the programme already: Mbewe, Isabel; Meltzer, Frances; Molefe, Tshepo; Moodley, Taralyn, Nkabine, Siyabonga Sipho; Saaymans, Martin Anthony; Sekhibane, Thandiwe Lerato.

And then I raise my phone, in landscape mode, and the image is grainy and shaky on the 10X telephoto zoom, as Silber, Sarah, is inducted as a Master of Science for her dissertation on *Behavioural correlates of stereotypic behaviour in Rhabdomys dilectus*, a species of striped mice.

At the end of the ceremony, back in their seats, the graduates wave their scrolls in the air, in recognition of their achievement and acknowledgement of the support of their families, their friends, their peers.

The congregation is dissolved, the academic procession leaves the hall, and after a beat of silence, a single word rises to the rafters.

'Wow!' And James Brown sings, 'I feel good, I knew that I would now,' as we file back into the sunshine.

Halala, Sarah-Jane; halala all the graduandi who will go out now and take their next step, and make their next mark on the world. And as the song reminds us, for now and for ever, vivat academia. Long live the academy!

Bra Hugh, the man who made some kind of noise

In 1984, the Johannesburg-based record company, Priority, crammed a bunch of music journalists into a minibus and put-putted them across the border to Botswana.

The occasion was a chat-and-listen session with the Master of Jazz, the Jazz Epistle, Bra Hugh Masekela, who had just finished recording an album called *Techno-Bush*, which would produce one of his biggest hits, the synth-driven dancefloor jam, 'Don't Go Lose It Baby'.

By the time we got to Gaborone, we were sweaty, tired, and aching from the rumble of the road. But we perked up when Bra Hugh emerged from his mobile studio, on the grounds of the Woodpecker Inn, wearing a long-trousered safari suit, brown loafers, and a cloth cap.

He pumped each of our hands in turn, and greeted us warmly in his famous sleepy-eyed drawl. He was amazed to learn that we had travelled five hours from Joburg to see him. 'Five hours?' he said. 'That's how long it takes me to get from Manhattan to Brooklyn in the morning!'

He had been living in exile for 22 years by then, in England, New York, and now Botswana, and had been on the road as a jazzman since the age of 16. He had been born in KwaGuqa, near Witbank, and had grown up in Springs, on the East Rand of Joburg. He must have felt the pang, because you could hear it in the call of his trumpet, of being so close yet so far away from home.

But when the question came up, during an impromptu conference around the swimming-pool, Bra Hugh shrugged it off with a wave of the hand. 'Even if things change,' he said, 'I don't think I'd move back down there.'

He mulled over it in the lazy sunshine. 'Maybe I'd get myself a little place on the coast, just to see why everyone goes to Durban in the Winter.'

He laughed, and then he gestured at the trees, the grass, the wide-open sky. 'I mean, I'm home,' he said. 'I have access to the music and the feeling. I couldn't ask for anything more.'

But within another six years, things would have changed: Mandela would be free, the first elections would be on the horizon, and Bra Hugh would be home, for good.

He stood on a rock for us, and he played his trumpet, blaring it into the heavens, accompanied only by the song of the birds. He thought about his friends and family back home, and he thought about his reasons for leaving, all those years ago.

'I just didn't want to die,' he said, 'without making some kind of noise.'

Rest in peace, Hugh Ramapolo Masekela. You made some kind of noise, and a whole lot of people, all around the world, are listening to it again today.

The Florentine Hustler of Silicon Valley

S teve Jobs, the iConic co-founder of Apple, whose memory will be evoked once again when the new range of iPhones is launched in San Francisco tonight, is widely regarded as a genius of modern technology.

And yet his genius, unlike that of his co-founder Steve Wozniak, was never technological in nature: he wasn't a programmer or an engineer or a designer or an inventor of things.

Rather, his genius was for making people believe, for re-aligning their reality field, for making them see the visions that were spinning and dancing in his head.

He was a master manipulator of emotion, a salesman, a marketer, a presenter, a teller and seller of stories that in some way were able to convince you that your life was about to change for the better.

There is a fine example of his strategy in *Valley of Genius*, an oral history of Silicon Valley, by Adam Fisher.

In 1990, in between his stints at Apple, Jobs was running a company called NeXT, whose prime product was a NeXT-level computer that was struggling to find a market.

In a bid to reverse its fortunes, Jobs wanted to recruit a senior marketing executive from Microsoft, Mike Slade, who had been instrumental in launching such hugely successful products as Excel, Works, and Microsoft Office.

So Jobs cornered Slade one day and told him: 'You're going to rot up there in Seattle,' a city as famous for its persistent rain as it was for being the home base of Microsoft. 'You know, Mike,' said Jobs, 'Palo Alto is a special place.'

He began selling Slade on an idealised vision of the city, in the sun-warmed heart of Silicon Valley, as an epicentre of creative energy, a hub of innovation, excitement and activity, where his talents would be able to blossom and flourish anew.

'Palo Alto is like Florence in the Renaissance,' said Jobs, and slowly, Slade began to believe. His field of reality shifted; he saw the visions in Jobs's head, as they crossed the line into his own. He signed up. He moved from Seattle. He started a new job with Jobs.

Then, one day, about a year later, Slade was sitting with his wife at a restaurant called Il Fornaio, on University Avenue in Palo Alto.

He was idly perusing the back of the menu, when a line in the blurb caught his eye. 'Palo Alto is like Florence in the Renaissance,' it read.

And there, almost word for word, as it continued, was the romantic, idealised spiel Jobs had sold him.

'The guy sold me a line from a menu!' marvelled Slade, recalling the story years later. 'From a chain restaurant! Bad ad copy from Il Fornaio, which was his favourite restaurant, right? Such a shameless bullshitter!'

And yet, of course, it worked, not because of the copy on the menu, but because Jobs knew, by heart and soul, how to harness and capture the primal emotion that underpins all marketing, all communication, all selling. We want to believe.

And when we encounter someone who is able to conquer our natural resistance, to cast aside the shield of our scepticism, just like that, in an instant, we are moved, and we are sold.

The Master of Whataboutery

Whataboutery is the art, in debate and dialogue, of evading a question by deflecting attention to an issue of supposedly equal or greater significance.

It is the easiest and cheapest of rhetorical tactics, dating all the way back to the schoolyard – 'I know I am, but what are you?' – which is why it is so beloved of politicians and their flock.

A current example can be found in the airing of the dirty laundering of monies allegedly paid by the embattled VBS Bank to the EFF's Floyd Shivambu, via his brother, Brian. YES, BUT WHAT ABOUT STEINHOFF?

In light of this, I was reminded today of a classic early example of whataboutery in South African politics, from Pik Botha, formerly Minister of Foreign Affairs in the National Party government.

Pik, who died today at the age of 86, had a certain Brylcreemed charm – he was, after all, a diplomat by training – but he could be brusque and combative in the public spotlight, particularly when faced with journalists who were trying to put him on the spot.

On this occasion, at the height of apartheid in the 1980s, he was being barbecued by an Australian television journalist, for a special on South Africa.

At one point, Pik misplaced his cool, leaned forward in his chair, and said, in that distinctive voice that sounded like a bakkie churning up gravel: 'What about the Aboriginals?'

This pretty much stunned the Australian into silence, since it is very hard to respond to whataboutery without getting all whataboutery yourself.

The catchphrase became instant fodder for satirists and

cartoonists, although it was eventually overshadowed by Pik's then-radical prediction, in another interview, that South Africa would one day have a black president.

Post-apartheid, Pik softened somewhat, and in 2000, he announced that he was going to become a member of the ANC.

As Pieter-Dirk Uys once famously said of Pik, who was a good-natured subject of his frequent lampooning: 'Pik Botha knows which side his bread is Bothaed.'

Mirabile dictu!

When I learned, while visiting the University of the Free State in Bloemfontein yesterday, that there was a student in the Journalism faculty who was studying Latin as an elective module, I thought, '*Mirabile dictu*! I've got to meet this guy.'

It's not that Latin, contrary to assumptions, is a dead language – it breathes every time we speak English – but it is increasingly rare to find anyone outside of the priesthood who pursues it, and even law students are no longer legally obliged to do so.

It was good, therefore, to chat with the lone classicist in question, Kopano Lekhoathi, who is in the second year of his BA (Journalism) degree.

I was on campus to share thoughts, ideas, and advice with students in the Communication Sciences, as part of the launch programme of the university's Industry Advisory Council (IAC), a panel drawn from members of various disciplines in media, marketing, and communication in general.

We discussed industry trends (I mentioned the rise of podcasting as a source of revenue and influence; 'slow news' as an antidote to the scourge of fake news; and algorithms replacing editors) and offered advice on what employers look for in candidates (I suggested broad general knowledge and curiosity about the world; savviness about social media practice and strategy; and an enthusiastic willingness to tackle tasks and assignments beyond the job spec).

Then we split into our separate speed-chatting stations, to

answer specific questions from the students, who were engaged and interested and bristling with bright-eyed ambition.

I was struck once again by how many young Journ students want to get into radio, or publish their books of poetry and fiction, or specialise in reporting on sport, entertainment, and the arts.

I always say: don't wait for the job to come your way; broadcast and publish and write today. Never before in the history of communication have so many platforms and opportunities been open to you.

Then I had a chat with Kopano. He told me how much he loves Latin, and how the strict discipline of declension and conjugation is helping to sharpen his English, and how he keeps coming across words in the Latin texts that have echoes and allusions in his mother tongue, Setswana.

'I can do minor translations,' he said, when I asked him about his level of conversational Latin. 'Safe to say I can distinguish between the nominative, vocative, accusative, and genitive cases.'

Suddenly I was back in high school Latin class myself, painstakingly conjugating verbs in cursive, and wondering how on earth the lingua franca of the ancient Romans would ever be of use to me in the modern world.

Kopano is a writer himself, of fantasy stories based on the Salem witchcraft trials in 17th century Massachusetts, and when I asked whether he was planning to practise journalism as a career, he said, 'I'd like to get experience as a journalist, but my main goal is to be a content creator.'

He also plans to study law as a postgraduate, and in the longer term, he hopes to become a filmmaker, or step into dance, perhaps, with his love of ballet, hip hop, and modern.

I asked Kopano where his interest in Latin comes from, and he smiled wistfully and said: 'Harry Potter is my childhood. Because of all the spells and that, I got interested in witchcraft, and then I thought, what is this language they are speaking? But I actually learn now that the language they are speaking for the spells is not 100 per cent Latin. It's a mixture of Italian and French as well. What I do is the Ecclesiastical Latin.'

In his smile, I saw the spark of connections, from Europe and England to the foot of Africa, from an ancient empire to a young democracy, from modern tales of wizardry and imagination to the poets, philosophers, and storytellers of antiquity.

I thought too of my father, a Latin scholar and teacher, who could converse as easily in Latin as in English, and who had a habit of loudly issuing declensions and conjugations around the household, for no other reason than that they sounded so magisterial.

Thank you, Kopano, and with all your studies, your endeavours, and your career, I wish you *Benediximus*!

My fok, Marelize

In the future, as the artist Andy Warhol almost said, every-body will be famous for 15 megabytes. For proof of this proposition, look no further than the moving tale of Marelize Horn, who was riding her bicycle on an otherwise deserted rugby field in Windhoek, Namibia, when she bumped smack-bang into an immovable object that momentarily halted her irresistible force.

The scientific explanation for why a cyclist, surrounded by empty space, would collide with a rugby goalpost, is a principle called 'target fixation', whereby one concentrates so hard on avoid-ing an object in one's path, that one hits it.

But it was the muttered reaction of young Marelize's mother, Heidi Horn, who was video-recording the cycle ride from a safe distance, that really made Marelize famous. 'My fok, Marelize,' she said, igniting an instant meme and a convenient expression of all-round exasperation, when the video hit the social networks.

This liedjie*, composed in Marelize's honour, is to be sung to the tune of 'Ironic', by Alanis Morissette. (Ironically, Marelize sent me a very sweet note on Facebook Messenger after the posting, when her exploit had rocketed her to the top of the fast-moving news cycle.)

It's like a power outage on your wedding day
It's like a TV licence that you're being threatened to pay
It's like trying to get to a meeting when you can't find your keys
It's My Fok, Marelize

It's like the Gautrain not running because of a strike
It's like a rugby post suddenly appearing in front of your bike
It's like trying to trace a parcel that was sent from overseas
It's My Fok, Marelize

It's like being out of warranty on a faulty appliance
It's like getting another SMS from the Democratic Alliance
It's like tripping on the pavement and grazing your knees
It's My Fok, Marelize

Sometimes the world just won't go your way
Sometimes you can't reach your goal
Sometimes you triumph on the field of play
And sometimes you bang into a pole

It's like having a braai and running out of beer
It's like designing a product and Woolworths stealing your idea
It's like someone ordering a pizza with pineapple on cheese
It's My Fok, Marelize

Sometimes you can't see the wood for the trees
Sometimes you wonder if you'll ever live a life of ease
The answer, my friend, is blowing in the breeze
It's My Fok, Marelize.

* With apologies, ironically, to Alanis Morissette, and Marelize.

Art is bull

Pablo Picasso, so the story goes, was strolling his way home one day, when he saw a pile of junk on the side of the road. He stopped to take a closer look.

To the artist, there is no junk; there is only art, waiting to be born. And there, amidst the tangled scrabble of discards, throwaways, and leave-behinds, he saw, in a flash of insight and imagination, an animal enshrined in myth, a noble beast, rising from the rusted skeleton of a bicycle.

In his studio, he welded the handlebars to the metal frame of the seat, creating, in that shower of sparks, one of the most iconic sculptures of the 20th century. *Tête de taureau*, or *Bull's Head*.

To say the work was not well received at its debut at the Salon d'Automne in Paris in 1944, when it was more prosaically catalogued as *Bicycle Seat*, would be an understatement.

The reaction from visitors, varying from derisive laughter to outright scorn, was so intense that it was removed from display.

Perhaps it looked too easy, too whimsical, this sculpture forged from found objects and a few flicks of the wrist. And yet, it was a symbol of a revolution.

Over the years, Picasso had obsessively sketched and painted bulls, capturing in fine and naturalistic detail their hulk, their sinew, their imposing strength. But here, he had reduced all of that to a minimalist fusion of metal and leather, shadow and light.

He had captured the essence of the bull, its spirit and flesh, and had discarded the rest. That is what art is, after all: it is what you are left with when you whittle away everything that isn't art. The hard part is knowing what to leave out, and why.

Today, Picasso's thinking is mirrored in the design process at Apple, where a selection of his works, the bulls in particular, is shown to designers as part of an internal training programme.

Look at the way Apple practises innovation by elimination, stripping away everything it believes isn't necessary to the better functioning and usability of its products.

Over the years, and often to the shock and chagrin of its customers, this has included the floppy-disk, the CD/DVD drive, the headphone-jack, the home-button, the physical phone-keyboard, and the USB port. What is left is what you need, at least in the vision of Apple.

Today, *Bull's Head* has pride of place at the Musée Picasso in Paris, and a big part of its enduring appeal is exactly its whimsicality, its ambiguity.

As you look at it, it shifts in your perception from a magnificent bull in repose, to a plain old bicycle seat and handlebars. Back and forth, back and forth.

Picasso called the work an act of metamorphosis, and he once spoke of his wish that the metamorphosis would occur in reverse: that someone would wander into a gallery, see it on the wall, and say, 'Ah! I need these for my bicycle!' before wandering off with the work.

Art, just like bits and pieces on a scrap-heap, will always have its uses, and even junk holds the power to spark joy, when seen in the right light.

The weaponisation of charm

Today I saw a news poster on a lamp-post – I get most of my news from lamp-posts these days – about the President's latest CHARM OFFENSIVE, in reference to his successful solicitation of billions of bucks in local and foreign investment at a summit in Sandton last week.

It's a lovely phrase, one of the great oxymorons of the modern era, and it has a sly streak of cynicism that can easily remain undetected if you aren't consciously mulling over it in the traffic.

The notion that charm can be a weaponisable commodity is integral to the battle to conquer hearts and minds, and is in fact the very working definition of Public Relations, particularly of the variety that gets politicians elected.

The genesis of the term can be traced to the early icicles of the Cold War, in October 1956, when the *Fresno Bee* quoted US General Alfred M Gruenther warning of the 'launching of the Russian charm offensive', and the consequent dangers of democracies relaxing their vigilance.

Since then, journalists have happily added the phrase to their arsenal of cliché, to be locked and loaded into action whenever a politician goes on a glad-handing, baby-kissing, teeth-flashing, podium-hugging, crowd-waving, selfie-grinning expedition, whether to garner votes, public confidence, or other people's money.

A quick Google revealed approximately 77 000 results for the phrase 'Cyril Ramaphosa charm offensive', although I stopped clicking after the first page, so I wouldn't be too sure about the accuracy of that figure.

Nonetheless, I believe we can all learn a lesson from the President, when it comes to deploying charm as an offensive tactic.

How much happier would we be on social media, for instance, if we could be charmed at the same time as we are offended by what people have to say.

'I am highly offended by your charm,' we could tweet. 'Kindly accept this tax-deductible contribution to your national invest-ment campaign.'

The happy-sad afterlife of Ricky Gervais

Pathos, in its dramatic meaning, is the ability to find the humour in pain and the pain in humour, and few performers are better at doing this than Ricky Gervais, who has crafted an unlikely career out of creating and portraying unlikeable characters.

Most notable, in the original UK version of *The Office*, is the pathologically chummy, petrochemically smarmy, self-obliviously offensive David Brent, a working model of the kind of working colleague the rest of us would cross the street to avoid, even if it meant getting knocked over by a pantechnicon in the process.

And yet, Brent is a barrel of awkward laughs compared to the character Gervais plays in his latest series, *After Life*, now streaming on Netflix.

Here we have a man, a stuck-in-a-rut small-town newspaper journalist by the name of Tony Johnson, who is gratuitously rude to everyone he meets, who mocks, taunts, and sneers at the physical attributes and belief systems of his workmates, who bluntly, coldly shatters the dreams of a bright-eyed newcomer to the profession, and who, in the manner of a mob hitman, threatens to use a hammer on a wide-eyed kid in a schoolyard.

But – and here's the kicker – we soon learn that Tony's greatest target, his greatest victim, is himself, as he battles to find a reason to be in the wake of the death of the one true love of his life, his wife, who we get to know through playful flashbacks and the home-video clips that he watches in sweet sadness on his laptop.

All of this may make *After Life* sound like grim, heavy going, but quite the contrary: it is a sharp, savagely funny, wise and ultimately life-affirming tragicom, and I can pinpoint the exact moment when I fell head-over-heels in love with it: at 1 minute and 7 seconds into the opening episode.

That was when Bill Withers began singing 'Lovely Day' on the soundtrack, as Tony drags himself out of bed and numbly goes about the routine of his suddenly lonesome existence.

The song is a winsome, blissful ode to radiant love, and it is a daringly counter-intuitive choice, because the obvious Withers song for the montage would have been its wintry opposite, 'Ain't No Sunshine'. All praise to Gervais for not falling into that trap.

Gervais was a musician before he became an actor-writer-director, and he uses music so well in this series, another highlight being the scene where he zones out on a couch, dragging on a joint to dull the pain, as Elton John's 'Rocket Man' lifts us high as a kite by then.

Gervais is the self-obsessed axis of the show, but the characters in his orbit, from the town junkie to the schlubby news photographer to the overworked old-age-home nurse to the widow he shares a bench with at the cemetery, are so convincingly real, so good at concealing their own aches and struggles, that we can only hope that some of their humanity will somehow rub off on him.

After Life, spanning six short episodes, is in essence a concise little parable of loss and redemption, and it reminded me of another now-classic tale of an abrasive, curmudgeonly misanthrope who eventually finds a reason to be: Bill Murray as the weatherbeaten weatherman in *Groundhog Day*.

You'll have to watch *After Life* for yourself to see how Tony handles his day-after-day-after-day, but here's the line and the lesson that lingers, as the final song plays to its fade-out: 'Happiness is amazing,' someone tells him at one point. 'It's so amazing, that it doesn't matter if it's yours or not.'

Goodnight, Opportunity

NASA/JPL-CALTECH/CORNELL ASU

It looks like static on a TV screen, a rush of random noise, scatterlings of electromagnetic energy quivering in the aftershock of the Big Bang.

But this is a signal of a different kind: a dispatch from the cold, dark surface of a faraway world.

The final image from the Mars rover, Opportunity, as it looks into the eye of a powerful dust-storm that has blocked out the sun.

The rover, 15 years into its mission to gather rocks and soil, and search for signs of life, on the red planet, transmits the image to NASA and begins shutting down its own systems to conserve power. But from this deep sleep, the Opportunity will never awaken.

Over many months, like Ground Control calling Major Tom, over and over and over, the engineers at NASA send a series of recovery commands to the bug-eyed, six-wheeled vehicle. But all they get back, across the eternal vastness of space, is silence. Finally, they send a song.

Billie Holiday, her languid vibrato soaring above the brooding piano and the muted trumpet: 'I'll find you in the morning sun, and when the night is new,' she sings, 'I'll be looking at the moon, but I'll be seeing you.'

And yet, for now, all we see is the void. What makes this such a haunting image is what it tells us about our own place in the cosmos, our own restless yearning to breach the barriers of what we know.

Those motes of light could just as easily be stars in a galaxy, or grains of sand, perhaps, waiting to be fired into the silicon crystals that power our phones and computers. Everything turns into dust; from dust, everything is born.

The first photograph the Opportunity sent back home, in 2004, was of its own shadow, its own ridged tracks in the Martian soil. A selfie.

The last is a photograph of nothing, and of everything. One day, many years from now, the machines and the robots having led the way, fragile beings of flesh and blood, the first interplanetary explorers, will follow in those tracks.

The dust will clear, the noise will stir into signal, and humanity will have found a new home. On earth, as it is amongst the stars, there is no lost opportunity.

Drifting off to sleep on a library of dreams

S ometimes, late at night, when I'm hovering on the edge of sleep
and I can't fall in, I lie there with my eyes closed and I start taking stock, not of sheep, but of famous Hollywood actresses.

It has to be actresses, in alphabetical order, by their first names:
don't ask me why. We all have our little rituals.

A for Audrey Hepburn (I picture her in *Breakfast at Tiffany's*).
B for Bette Davis, with her eyes and cigarette smouldering in *All
About Eve*. C for Charlize Theron, in her breakthrough role as
Helga in 2 *Days in the Valley*. D for Demi Moore, with her Navy
Seal buzz-cut in *G.I. Jane*. E for Elizabeth Taylor, in *Cat on a Hot
Tin Roof*. F for Faye Dunaway, in *Bonnie & Clyde*, of course. G
for … zzz.

By this time, I am fast asleep, plummeting into the abyss on
flickering wings of silvery light. There is something about the act
of cataloguing from memory, of dredging names and faces from
the deep, that stirs up the sandman's silt from the muddy waters.

But lately, I have found an even surer way of applying for my visa
to dreamland. I count books.

Not just any books, and not many books: the whole idea is to
winnow down your hoard to a few truly resonant and meaningful
titles, in line with the life-advice from Marie Kondo, the world's
foremost tidying-up expert, who restricts her own collection to
no more than 30 volumes at a time, according to her new book,
*Spark Joy: An Illustrated Master Class on the Art of Organizing
and Tidying Up*.

This figure of 30 is entirely moot, first of all because it is based on just one person's ideal of a less-cluttered, more orderly universe, and secondly because books no longer exist purely on the physical plane.

One of the things I like most about the age we live in, is that I can carry my entire library around on my phone, without the books taking up space or gathering dust on a shelf. Still, it's a useful thought-exercise, on the edge of sleep, to wonder which titles you would keep, if you could only keep 30.

I usually only get to 10 or so, before the effort sends me nodding off. But it's a pleasant effort. Recounting old books is like having old friends around for tea, especially if, being good friends, they have brought with them the old books you foolishly lent them many years ago.

Last night I started my catalogue with *The Wonderful Wizard of Oz*, by L Frank Baum. It was the first 'big book' I ever read, having breezed my way through all the Blytons, and I remember thinking, when Dorothy and Toto were safely back in Kansas, that I would never in my life read a book more wonderful and enchanting than this. I still think I was right.

Then I moved on to Lewis Carroll's *Alice's Adventures in Wonderland*, the annotated version by Martin Gardner, with footnotes that lead you down a rabbit-hole of mind-altering revelations, including this suggested answer to the Mad Hatter's riddle: Why is a raven like a writing-desk? Answer: Because there is a B in both.

And so on and on, from *A Clockwork Orange* by Anthony Burgess to *Catch-22* by Joseph Heller, from *Rebecca* by Daphne du Maurier to *Slaughterhouse-Five* by Kurt Vonnegut, from *The Catcher in the Rye* by JD Salinger to *The Meaning of Liff* by Douglas Adams, from *The Family of Man*, the photographic collection curated by Edward Steichen, to *Archy & Mehitabel* by Don Marquis, from Mary Shelley's *Frankenstein* to my favourite novel from last year, *My Year of Rest and Relaxation* by Ottessa Moshfegh, which, incidentally, is about someone who takes a year off from the chaos of the world to sleep.

By that time, I was sound asleep, thanks to books and Marie Kondo.

Where I do take issue with her advice, and she has a lot to say about books in her book, is where she suggests that books should be discarded once they have been read.

'We read books because we seek the experience of reading,' she writes. 'Once read, a book has already been "experienced".'

To me, reading is just the mechanical act, the process of absorbing data through the transfer of symbols to the cerebellum.

The reason we read books is not to experience reading – that novelty tends to wear off in the early years of schooling – but to experience life, in all its happenings and moods and emotions, and to see and maybe understand the world and worlds beyond, through the eyes and lives of others.

Books are particles of the heart. That is why we hold onto books we've already read, and why we re-read them over the years, not because they will have changed, but because we have, and because books, once read, have a way of weaving themselves into our dreams.

The fleet-footed rising of a new dawn

I was running a race last night – all right, I was walking a race, ambling and dawdling at the back of the pack, where you get cheered on the loudest by the spectators lining the street – so I missed the live transmission of the new State President's State of the Nation Address.

But I did think about the State of the Nation a lot, because the annual Randburg Harriers' Valentine's Night Race, winding for 10 kilometres through the suburban streets of Randburg, always has the celebratory feel of a Big South African Event, like the day Bafana Bafana won, or the day the Boks won, or the day everyone stood in a queue for the first time to vote.

I think the image that most summed up the race for me, in between the whooping and the ululating and the parping of vuvuzelas, and the jazz band with their music stands playing 'Summertime' in the hot night air, was the oke sitting on a camping chair outside his house, one leg draped over the armrest, the national flag flying high on a pole next to him, the boerewors sizzling on the gas-braai behind, raising a bottle of Castle in his hand, and shouting, over and over again: 'Almost there! Come on, you're almost there!'

In South Africa, we are almost always almost there, some of us running, some of us shuffling, some of us making a noise on the sidelines, and last night, in Parliament, the President took us a couple of steps closer to wherever it is we're going.

The full speech is now online, so I had a good look at it, and on the surface, it is very business-like, a telling of accomplishments and a foretelling of plans and promises, and in this way, it is not too different in tone and style from a corporate annual report, of which Cyril Ramaphosa has surely delivered plenty in his business career.

But a good political speech cannot be business alone, as Aristotle made clear, a couple of thousand years ago, in his guidelines for persuasive rhetoric. He said good oratory must be built on a combination of Ethos, a call to credibility and authority, Logos, a call to logic, and Pathos, a call to emotion.

It is the pathos we remember, the ringing, stirring phrases, the touchstones of the heart, long after the ethos and the logos have been consigned to history.

With this in mind, Ramaphosa's speech echoes some of the most resonant political speeches in history, so that we hear them, almost subliminally, between the lines.

When the President says, 'We are building a country where a person's prospects are determined by their own initiative and hard work, and not by the colour of their skin', he is echoing MLK's 'I Have a Dream' ('that my four little children will one day live in a nation where they will not be judged by the colour of their skin'); when he declares that 'no nation can be free until its women are free', he is echoing Lenin's declaration that 'No nation can be free when half the population is enslaved in the kitchen'; when he promises that 'a new dawn is upon us', he is echoing the most famous line in 'The Regeneration of Africa', a speech by the founder and former President of the ANC, Pixley ka Isaka Seme, all the way back in 1906: 'The brighter day is rising upon Africa'.

There are echoes, too, of Thabo Mbeki's own 'I Am an African', of Nelson Mandela's 'Free at Last', and right at the end, in the most striking use of pathos in the speech, of JFK's inaugural address in 1961: 'Ask not what your country can do for you, ask what you can do for your country.'

Here lies the real emotive power of Ramaphosa's speech, in its quoting of nine lines from 'Thuma Mina', by the recently departed Hugh Masekela.

The song's gospel-influenced refrain, 'I wanna lend a hand, send me', becomes, in Ramaphosa's closing words, an echo of a former ANC campaign slogan: 'Now is the time to lend a hand. Now is the time for each of us to say, "send me".'

Thus, is a hashtag born; thus, is the power of the President devolved to the power of every person in the street; thus, will this speech be remembered, not for its long list of plans and pledges, but for its passing of the baton, on the brink of a new dawn, to each and every one of us who runs or walks the race, at whatever pace, in whatever colours we fly. We're almost, almost there.

Thirty sows and pigs

On note-taking:

I do not record. I've never recorded. I'm a very fast note-taker. When someone kind of says the "it" thing that I have really wanted, I don't start scribbling right away. I have an almost photographic memory and so I wait a beat or two while they're onto something else, and then I write down the previous thing they said. Because you don't want your subject to get nervous about what they just said.

This confession by Jill Abramson, the former executive editor of *The New York Times*, whose chequered career also includes stints as an investigative reporter on *The Wall Street Journal* and as political columnist for *The Guardian*, has had Journalism Twitter in a tizz today. I feel pretty tizzy about it myself.

I mean, talk about Old School – a journalist who still uses paper and pen to take notes during interviews! Not that there's anything wrong with paper and pen, although I've never known a journalist who had a pen handy when you need to borrow one.

Me, I feel completely lost without some or other recording device on the table. It's not just the warm buzz of security you get from knowing you are recording every word for posterity and the settling of future arguments over who said what – it's the knowledge that you are getting every word down in its context, in all its colloquial nuance, in its exact inflection and semantic precision.

So often during an interview – which is really just a slightly more formal form of conversation – what you think you heard someone say, turns out to be something subtly but crucially different when you go back and re-listen to it.

Of course, ideally you should pause and ask for clarity at the very moment, but it's not always feasible or easy to do this.

So later on, you hit rewind and you turn up the volume and you listen carefully, over and over, until – aha! – you hear it right.

The most famous example of a mishearing by a journalist is that of the Australian rural correspondent who reported that 30 000 pigs had been swept away in a flood, when in fact, the farmer had said '30 sows and pigs'.

Careful listening to a recording thereof, combined with a working knowledge of animal husbandry, might have spared the journo the global embarrassment that followed.

In any case, we have reached an era of technological advancement where it is a trivial matter to record a conversation. Just tap the app on your phone. The quality, in my experience, is more than good enough to capture an interview, even in a fairly noisy setting.

Having said that, I do very much admire journalists of the Jill Abramson ilk, who are confident enough of their ability not only to remember what has been said, but to capture it live, with all the speed and accuracy required of their profession.

And more than anything, who are organised enough to remember to bring a working pen and a notebook with sufficient blank pages along to an interview.

'Si swirt sweeu see sweep swip tsik'

I was five minutes early for a meeting this morning – I always try to be five minutes early for a meeting – so I parked, switched off the car, and idly thumbed through my Twitter feed to pass the time.

Suddenly, there came a tapping, as of someone gently rapping, to mis-quoth Edgar Allen Poe, rapping at my rolled-up window.

This is Joburg, so my first impulse was to sit up with a skrik and look to the source of the sound. My second impulse was to reach, very slowly, for my phone, flip it to camera mode, and: snap.

The bird carried on tapping, as if annoyed that the air had mysteriously turned solid, making, as it did so, a high-pitched noise that I can only describe as a 'tweet'.

Then it flew off, its long tail sweeping as it swooped into the branches. I sent a quick dispatch to the family WhatsApp group.

'What kind of bird is this?' I enquired. 'He wanted to get into the car.'

Within seconds came an answer from an expert ornithologist on the group. 'OMG cute!!! It's an orange-billed sparrow.'

That sounded reasonable enough to me, but a counter-offer swiftly followed from another expert ornithologist on the group.

'That is NOT an orange-billed sparrow.' I could almost hear the flipping of the much-leafed pages as the *Roberts* was hauled out of storage and consulted.

Finally: 'It's a pin-tailed whydah. Common resident in open savannah. Goes "Si swirt sweeu see sweep swip tsik".' All right, then. Not 'tweet'.

The bird – the pin-tailed whydah, to be precise – returned, this time tapping red-beakedly at its own reflection in the, ahem, wing-mirror, like Robert De Niro talking to himself in *Taxi Driver*.

Then it flew away again, and I opened the door and stepped into the open savannah of suburban Johannesburg, looking anxiously into the skies before I rushed into my meeting, with barely a minute to spare.

The day One-Shot Mike shot Annie, the Queen of the World

I have a bunch of ancient copies of *Style* magazine scattered around my study, waiting to trip me up as a reminder to organise and catalogue them at some point.

They are time capsules of a golden – or at least, a gilt-edged – era in South African magazine journalism, characterised by conspicuous consumption, social climbing, and sly satire of the fears and foibles of our largely well-to-do target market.

Today this issue, from September 1987, caught my eye, and as I flipped through it, it made me think once again of how the world has changed, in very many ways for the better, in some ways not. Let me tell you a little story about the not. That's Anneline Kriel on the cover.

In 1974, at the Royal Albert Hall in London, she was crowned first runner-up in the Miss World pageant. But only four days later, the title-holder, Helen Morgan of the UK, resigned and handed in her sash and tiara, after the tabloids discovered, to their feigned shock-horror, that she was an unwed mother.

Technically, this wasn't against the arcane and rigid rules of the competition, but the Miss World Organization, seeking to preserve their own reputation as arbiters and purveyors of an even-then-antiquated ideal of feminine grace and beauty, put pressure on her to quit. So she did, and Anneline stepped up to become the new Miss World.

Even years after her reign, she continued to exert a magnetic pull on the South African media. She had glamour enough to light up a room just by walking into it, in the flashbulb-popping manner of Old Hollywood.

One day, my editor at *Style*, Marilyn Hattingh, asked me to spend a day in Anneline's company, a prospect at which I first rolled my eyes, since I pretentiously fancied myself as being more at home on the grittier side of Joburg life.

But then I learned that the assignment would involve a day filled with watching Anneline shooting a TV commercial for Beacon chocolate, and I thought, ooh, okay, chocolate.

When I got to the studio in the north of Joburg, Anneline was lounging on a chaise of the blackest, plushest leather, with a creamy velvet curtain as the backdrop. It was swirled in the shape of a hammock, and it looked like melted chocolate in mid-pour.

Anneline's hair, in the style of the era, was a starburst of honey-spun blonde, and she was wearing a strapless black cocktail dress, just above knee-height, as one does, I assumed, when eating chocolate on a chaise lounge.

She had a tiny square pertly poised between thumb and forefinger, and she was rehearsing her lines, with her drama coach watching. He was leaning forward intensely, just in front of the glass-topped coffee-table with its vase of swooning, flame-petalled tulips.

'So smooth, so creamy. It's much too smooth to bite,' said Anneline, half-closing her eyes, lifting the chocolate closer to her lips. 'Just let it melt slowly in your mouth. And that smooth creaminess …'

And so it went, on and on, take after take, unwrapped chocolate bar after unwrapped chocolate bar, beneath the swelter of the lights, the dust of makeup in the air, the crew going about their toil with military precision, all in the quest to sway South

Africans, as the marketing director earnestly told me, from the 'colonial Britishness' of traditional chocolate to the more refined and sophisticated continental palate of Beacon.

Towards the end of the day, the plan was that we would steal some of Anneline's time to shoot a cover for the mag.

The commissioned photographer was a guy named Mike McCann, who was a hard-news shooter by trade and instinct, and who arrived, as he always did, on his racing bicycle, which he propped against a wall before striding in, with the bicycle clips still gleaming on his trouser cuffs.

'Howzit, Annie!' he called out, lifting his Leica M4, the preferred tool of the serious photojournalist, much-used in combat zones and in candid street portraiture. Annie looked up from the couch.

'Haai, Mike!' she smiled, her eyes lighting up, her delectable Witbank accent still blissfully unaffected by her travels across the world. Mike took a quick look at the setup, and he said to Annie the word so beloved of photographers who know and love their craft: 'Beautiful.' She looked at him. He put the Leica to his eye.

'Turn your head to me, Annie,' he said, 'a little more this way … that's it … just raise your shoulder a bit … ah. Perfect.' And he touched the shutter, which whispered with a metallic 'ksk', as Leica shutters do, and he smiled and waved at Annie, and he walked out and got back on his bicycle.

I just stood there, stunned. One shot? For a cover? I was about to ask Mike whether he shouldn't shoot some more, just for safety, but he was gone, and I was fearful that my editor would berate me in the morning for letting him get away like that, but he was Mike McCann, and she wasn't at all surprised.

This was the cover. It glows with the natural beauty of available light, and the slight graininess of 35 mm film, and in capturing Annie's glamour, I think Mike captured some of her heart and soul too.

There is no way on earth, in the era of digital photography, that a photographer would dare to shoot, just once, like this, for a glossy magazine, but Mike had an abiding confidence and enough trust in his own abilities to know what he needed to do to get exactly what his editor wanted.

Those days are gone forever, but the image lingers, in a frozen moment of connection that sings across the ages.

Skabenga, the King of Cats

Skabenga, the famous housecat-in-residence at the Oyster Box Hotel in Umhlanga, assists with a check-in today, by turning his back on the checker-inner and blithely ignoring the rather obvious mouse just to his right.

Skabenga – a mangling of the isiZulu term, S'gebengu, meaning 'vagabond' or 'hooligan' – is a former feral who worked his way up to adulation and celebrity, much like the subject of the wistful 1960s pop ballad, 'Where Do You Go To, My Lovely', which is about a prima donna who takes pains to hide her humble origins.

Skabenga, however, has nothing to hide, partly because his size makes it difficult for him not to be seen, and partly because such concerns are moot, given that all felines are regal by birth.

When we first chanced upon Skabenga, he was lolling slothfully in the lobby of this opulent establishment, his repose reminiscent of the Emperor Nero in the last days of Rome.

Skabenga magnanimously accepted a pat on the head, although his Churchillian scowl made it plain that he was not to be distracted from his duties, chief of which is to stand Skabengally – all right, repose Skabengally – for everything that the Oyster Box represents.

Skabenga is the hotel's official emissary, and his sullen visage, framed by his diamanté bell-collar, can be seen on T-shirts, party balloons, boxes of special-brew tea, and a myriad of souvenirs in the hotel's shop.

Skabenga has his own Facebook page and he is also the star of a children's book about his exploits.

He is frequently mentioned in dispatches on TripAdvisor ('All this … and Skabenga too!' reads a typically enthusiastic review) and the hotel treats him to an annual birthday bash which helps to raise funds for charity.

The wonderful animal-affairs site, The Dodo, featured Skabenga under the headline 'Africa's Grumpiest Cat Has the Best Life Ever', and its selection of pictures included one that I think really sums up Skabenga's personality and position.

It shows him perching proprietarily on the red carpet at the Oyster Box, as Manchester United players walk watchfully past him, acknowledging the cheers and waves of a group of onlookers who, let's be honest about this, were quite clearly really cheering and waving at Skabenga.

If you're ever in Umhlanga, be sure to pop in to the Oyster Box and make his majestic acquaintance for yourself.

Skitching a ride

I was strolling down Regent Road in Sea Point the other day, minding everybody else's business, when I saw this dude with the skateboard skating as fast as a MyCiTi bus.

That's because he was holding on to the back of a MyCiTi bus while skating, a practice technically known as 'skitching', or hitching while riding a skateboard.

There is a famous scene in the first *Back to the Future* movie, in which Michael J Fox, while skateboarding, grabs on to the back of a pickup truck and skitches to get away from a bunch of bullies who are chasing him in their car.

Rounding a corner, he back-foots the skateboard, and sparks fly from its metal tail. Back in the present, here on Regent Road, sparks flew too.

The air was dented by a short, sharp whoop, the unmistakable siren song of official admonition, and I turned to see a traffic patrol car approaching at speed.

There was a second, more insistent whoop, at which the skateboarder detached himself from the back of the bus, and sailed to the sidewalk with the cool grace of an ice-skater completing a routine.

I had never seen a skateboarder being pulled over by the cops before, so I lingered awhile to watch the negotiations, which did not appear to go favourably for the skateboarder.

Unsurprisingly, as is the case in many cities, skateboarding on a public road is against the law in Cape Town, specifically the

By-law Relating to Streets, Public Places and the Prevention of Noise Nuisances of 2007, sub-section 15 of which advises that 'No person shall on a public road skate on roller-skates or a skate-board or similar device except where permitted by the City.'

The 'except' part of that clause suggests a certain capacity for compromise, and a few years ago, the city began working with a lobby group called the National Skateboarding Collective to find ways of integrating skateboarding as a mode of transport in the city.

One of the outcomes of these sessions was the construction of the Gardens Skate Park, under the Mill Street/Jutland Avenue Bridge, which, interestingly, is situated right next to a MyCiTi bus stop.

Nonetheless, perhaps because Cape Town is blessed with such long downhills (and indeed, such long uphills), the city's streets themselves remain popular with skateboarding-bylaw breakers, a prime example being a guy by the name of Décio Lourenço, who in 2013 triggered a speed-camera trap while rocketing down Kloof Nek Road one morning at a recorded speed of 110 km/h, on a skateboard, powered only by gravity and his own feet.

Skateboarding, which began as an informal form of urban surf-ing in California in the 1940s, has become an integral element of street culture around the world, and its occasionally unsteady road to mainstream acceptance and respectability has led it all the way to Tokyo in 2020, where it will make its formal debut as an Olympic sport.

The best skateboarders are artists, athletes, conjurers, Zen phi-losophers of the wide-open road, and yet, as this little incident proved to me, among the many lessons we can learn from the prac-titioners of the lifestyle and the sport, is that there must, surely, be safer ways of catching a MyCiTi bus.

'I'm not Charlie!'

At about 4.30 pm yesterday, an urgent message was sent out on the WhatsApp groups and Facebook community groups in my neighbourhood in northwestern Joburg.

A 12-year-old boy named Charlie, who has autism, had gone missing from his home in the suburb of Quellerina. 'He is most probably on a white bicycle,' said the message, along with a detailed description and contact numbers.

Immediately, people sprang into action across a wide area, spanning several suburbs, with a busy freeway in between. Security companies joined in the search, working together with members of Community Policing Forums, or CPFs.

In total, more than 60 private patrol vehicles were involved in the street-by-street search, as the sky darkened with the promise of a late-afternoon Highveld storm.

Little bits of advice streamed in – 'Look in trees, he's a climber'; 'No, he does not have a cellphone'; 'If anyone does spot him, please tell him in Afrikaans that he must stay with you' – as well as reports of sightings along the way.

Someone announced on WhatsApp that a search party was going to be meeting at the BP garage in Bergbron. Someone else, from a suburb far outside the area, offered to coordinate a mountain-biking group with bike lights to 'search all the trails'.

The sky grew darker, the prayer emojis more frequent. Then, at 6.06 pm came the news: the missing boy had been found, safe and sound, near a church in Newlands, about 5 km from his home. That's quite a cycle ride.

But more than that, it's proof positive of the power of social networking to bring people together in a common cause. In days gone by, it would have taken a huge effort, and a coordinated information campaign on print and electronic media, just to get the message out.

Now, it goes out in seconds, as status updates are copied and pasted and shared across multiple groups and platforms. Then people respond, neighbours, family, friends and strangers, all looking out, all trying to help, all going out of their way to solve a crisis.

Social networks, and social networking groups, are often criticised for bringing out the worst in people, and there is some truth to that; but the greater truth, and it is demonstrated and proved over and over again, is that they are equally capable of bringing out the best.

But my favourite anecdote of the day came via a Facebook post from one of the searchers, who said: 'There was a kid cycling on a bike around Bergbron, and when I stopped to ask him if he had seen anything, he just screamed, "I'm not Charlie!"'

James Phillips, the great nobody of South African music

J ames Phillips, his face framed by a cascade of unruly curls, making him look, for all the world, like a Renaissance painter's vision of the martyred Saint Sebastian, curls his lip in contemplation, momentarily flummoxed by an off-camera question from his interviewer.

It is the ultimate question, an existential challenge, even if it is really just meant as a cue for a quick introduction: say who you are.

'Ah well, I can't really say who I am,' says James, and a flicker of a smile crosses his face, before vanishing like a wisp of smoke. 'I'm just a name. A voice from the void.' And then he stares straight ahead, and you wait for the laugh, but he keeps it deadpan, the master of irony, the master of pastiche, the master of the meaningful pause.

Thus begins *The Fun's Not Over*, the brilliant, illuminating, and deeply moving new documentary by Michael Cross, exploring the too-short life and times of James Phillips, singer-songwriter-musician, prophet without profit in his own country, reluctant mainstay of the Voëlvry alternatiewe Afrikaner musiek movement, and restless quester for the crafting of an authentic South African rock voice at the cusp of our transition to democracy.

Like the Radio Rats, the subject of Michael's joyously tender earlier ode to rock 'n roll dreamers, *Jiving and Dying*, James hailed from Springs, the East Rand mining town where there isn't much to do but hail, and the louder, the better.

He was the son of a pastor, a lineage that puts him in the same flock 'n roll category as Alice Cooper, Marvin Gaye, and the Kings of Leon. By the time he was a teenager, playing Bob Dylan covers at the Methodist Church Hall on an outsize Jumbo steel-string guitar, as Radio Rat Jonathan Handley recalls, it was already clear that James wasn't going to follow in his dad's pastoral footsteps.

But he did in a sense become a preacher, using music to fill the void, and to lend rhythm and meaning to his naïve conviction that even in the darkest and most brutal days of the mid-1980s, the light of a better day shone somewhere ahead.

'It's my duty to sing songs to my fellow South Africans,' we hear James saying, in one of many interview clips that are threaded through the movie. 'Hopefully we'll have a better image of ourselves in the future, liking ourselves and our culture.'

What a Jamesian irony, then, that in a bid to carve a place for himself in that nascent, simmering culture, he flirted most closely with fame by erasing his own identity, his own name, to become a literal nobody: Bernoldus Niemand, in whose alter-ego, with the lip of a Stetson masking his face, he sang the rollicking military-conscript drinking song, 'Hou My Vas, Korporaal'.

Instantly catchy, rough-edged, slyly subversive, the ditty was purpose-written to rise to the top of the Springbok Radio Hit Parade, in an era when overtly and even covertly political records were routinely scratched with a nail on their vinyl surface, to prevent them from ever being played by the SABC's rigidly monitored deejays. So that little dream, alas, didn't come true.

But even today, the lyrics resonate, and when Bernoldus sings 'Dis nie my skuld, maar ek hou my bek' – it's not my fault, but I keep my mouth shut – it is as wrenching an admission of passive complicity as pastor Martin Niemöller's famous poem, 'First They Came'.

There is so much to think about in this movie, so much to listen to, from the tight, kicking punk of James's first four-piece,

Corporal Punishment, to the raw, boozy rock of The Cherry Faced Lurchers, to the mellow, yearning piano ballads that James put to bed in the final days before he died of complications from a motor vehicle accident in July 1995. He was only 36 years old.

What lingers, for me, in his legacy, is the silences as much as the music, because James was classically trained, with a B.Mus from Wits, and he knew the dramatic and poetic virtues of the rest, the pause, the stop – whether used for comic effect, as in 'Toasted Takeaways' by The Lurchers, where the song would suddenly halt to allow the audience to shout out their orders for takeaways, or the chilling, gut-punching effect in his most powerful song, 'Shot Down in the Streets', where the stop feels like a gunshot suspended in negative space.

'Shot Down' has a hymnal quality, reflecting James's upbringing as well as his re-embracing of Christianity, during a period where he called himself James the Boptist and testified: 'I must tune you I'm one-way full on praising the Lord, ek sê.'

But it is not a song of redemption or salvation; it is a song of lurching and stumbling to one's knees, as the final rush of lyrics reminds us: 'I'm a white boy who looked at his life gathered in his hands, and saw it was all due to the sweat of some other man, that one who got shot down in the street.'

We are all, for better or worse, what we are because of other people, and in the end, as in the beginning, the voice in the void comes through loud and clear, in the way the movie gives James his due and calls on us to join him on his remarkable journey.

The Fun's Not Over is a happy-sad masterpiece of South African musical lore. Deep, funny, and engaging, it shines a powerful light on one man's creative journey, in a nation that is always on the edge of chaos, and always, as James hoped and knew in the heart of his music, on the threshold of better days ahead.

Sorry, hey

This poster, displayed at various beach-points along the promenade in Sea Point, is a masterpiece of human-friendly design, even if, in the process, it is inherently unfriendly to dogs.

With deftness of line, boldness of colour, and creative use of negative space, it turns a public-bylaw notice into a work of art.

The style is reminiscent of the 'cut-out' technique of the French Post-Impressionist, Henri Matisse, and the sans-serif typography also brings the crisp, authoritative clarity of London tube hoardings to mind.

If I have any criticism at all, it is that the upper dog is not strictly necessary, given the strength of the woe-is-me pose of the main dog, which perfectly communicates the message at a single glance.

Personally, also, I would be tempted to add a 'hey' at the end of the sorry, just to add an extra touch of South Africanness to the ag-shame injunction: 'Sorry, hey.'

Otherwise, I salute the designer, and am pleased to report that at a beach just a little further up from this poster, there is a poster of similar design, showing a dog leaping in the air below the legend 'Dogs Allowed at all times'.

The song that made the walls come tumbling down

Last night, Rachel invited a few friends over for a get-together in the garden, and as always, I obeyed the Unspoken Rule of such events, which is: No Boomers Allowed.

Still, I couldn't help hearing the music that seeped through the wall that divided the generations, and for the most part it seeped through my ears too, a muffled coagulation of thuds and thumps that occasionally mutated into a chorus.

This is the way it always sounds when you are distant from a party: the music breaks down into its nuclear components, and because music is mostly rhythm, it is the rhythm section that you hear, the hammering of the drums and the depth-charges of the bass, above and below everything else.

But then, as the evening wore on, there came a point when I heard the trill of a piano and the lonely wail of a blues harp, and in the sweep of that overture, I could hear the words of the opening verse before I even heard them: 'It's nine o'clock on a Saturday, the regular crowd shuffles in,' crooned Billy Joel, and the thing that amazed me was that he wasn't crooning alone.

Rachel and her friends were singing along, word-perfect, as if they were in that piano bar in, what was it, 1974? 1975? 1973?

'Sing us a song, you're the piano man,' they sang, louder and louder, their voices reeling into the night, 'we're all in the mood for a melody, and you've got us feeling alright ...'

The wall had shattered now, crumbled into dust, and while I was still compelled to obey the injunction – I couldn't run into the garden and sing along, even when the next song turned out to be

'American Pie' – I could feel the strands of connection, between the memories of one generation and the discoveries of the next.

Later that evening, when everyone had left, I complimented Rachel on her playlist, and she said, what playlist? The playlist with 'Piano Man' and 'American Pie', I said, and slowly, the strands began to unravel.

In the widening of the cultural gulf, I realised I was still thinking of music as something that required a physical delivery mechanism, a needle lowered onto a groove, a play-button pressed on a tape-deck or a CD player.

In that model, if you have people over for a get-together, you command the mechanism as well as the music: you are the taste-dictator, imposing your selection on the gathering, and assuming, because you have such impeccable taste, that they will be happy with it.

But Rachel and her friends, well, they each have a world of music on them, on Spotify or Apple Music or YouTube, and they share it, taking turns to stream their choice of songs through Bluetooth, WiFi, or the aux cable.

This is music as democracy, as community, as collaboration, and this is as music should be, a force that lives and breathes in the ether and is available to be summoned at a touch.

'Oh!' I said, as Rachel rolled her eyes, but there was still one burning question that I had to ask. 'How did you all know "Piano Man"? That's a song from the Seventies!'

The question bounded back at me, like a boomerang. 'Who doesn't know "Piano Man"?' said Rachel, and of course she was right.

There is a famous story about Billy Joel, that he was walking with his teenage daughter in New York one day, and because he was Billy Joel and because it was New York, he burst all of a sudden into song. And she ran away from him, her hands over her ears, mortified with embarrassment.

The Boomers will always embarrass the Millennials – that is their lot in life – but when the music begins to play, if it is the right song at the right moment, the walls between us will crumble, and everyone, in their own way, will sing along.

The trouble with political jokes is that they get elected

The recent victory of a stand-up comedian in Ukraine's Presidential elections is all the proof the world needs that voters are able to take a joke, and elect it all the way to high office.

The punchline here, in one of history's greatest examples of life imitating showbiz, is that President-elect Volodymyr Zelensky has absolutely no previous experience of politics, unless you count his role as a high school teacher who gets elected President of Ukraine in the sitcom series, *Servant of the People*.

Hail to the Chief, I say, given how notoriously tough it is to win hearts and minds in the gruelling gladiatorial arena of the comic arts.

Anyone who is brave enough to stand in the spotlight will be subjecting themselves to the firing-squad of public opinion, but only a stand-up will measure the success of their performance on whether they 'killed' or 'died' on stage.

For an hour or two at a time, typically with no props other than a microphone, a bar-stool, and a glass of water, the stand-up must riff from topic to topic, observation to anecdote, commanding our attention with a stream-of-consciousness flow that makes us think, makes us recognise ourselves, and makes us, every now and again, laugh.

This is a delicate balance, like tap-dancing on razor-wire, and for it to work, the danger must ideally be felt in the audience too.

There are many genres of stand-up, from family-friendly to absurdist to profane, but my personal favourite has always been the dark, morbid, and misanthropic variety, where the stand-up seduces us away from our safe spaces, leads us to the edge of the abyss, and pushes us in, to the echoing of our own laughter.

The effect is cathartic and often oddly invigorating, given how such comedy, as in the case of George Carlin and Ricky Gervais, can act as a veneer for a defiantly humanist approach to life.

I would vote for such a comedian in a heartbeat, even if Carlin's own advice on voting was an unequivocal 'don't'. (He believed voters only have themselves to blame when things go horribly wrong.)

Either way, the chief difference between a stand-up comedian and a politician is that stand-ups are better at lying, their secret weapon being a confidence trick that the ancient Greeks called the paraprosdokian, or the misdirection, as it is more commonly known.

Let me give you an example, from the new Netflix special by Anthony Jeselnik, *Fire in the Maternity Ward*. At one point, the lanky, leather-jacketed Jeselnik begins spinning a wistful tale from the banks of childhood memory.

'When I was a little kid,' he says, 'I had a pet turtle. Tiny little turtle. Kept him in an aquarium. One Summer, I went away to camp.'

We know where this is going. Or at least, we think we do. When he gets back from camp, the kid's father tells him a little lie: 'Anthony, your turtle is alive and well. It just went to go live with your mother.'

Then comes the paraprosdokian, the hard-left turn into an alternative reality.

'I believed that until a couple days later,' says Jeselnik. 'I was digging around in the backyard … and found my mom's body. Worst day of my life. I loved that turtle.'

The secret thrill of stand-up comedy is that we, the audience, give the stand-up permission to say the unsayable, while they, in turn, give us permission to laugh at the unlaughable.

That is as true a definition of democracy in progress as ever there was, and thanks to President-elect Zelensky, we now know that it applies in the political arena too.

Which is why I, for one, look forward to putting it to the test, as I stand proudly in line for my free Wimpy coffee on Election Day.

The whip-crack symphony of a night in the suburbs

Last night, a quiet suburban night in Northcliff, Johannesburg, split by the pop-pop-pop of … firecrackers? No, wait: Guy Fawkes is still a couple of weeks away, and this volley is sharper, louder, with the crack of a whip in its tail.

And then, the roar of a vehicle slamming into gear, and the sickening crescendo of the crash, the shattering of glass and the twisting of metal, and then, silence.

Within seconds, the first messages appear on the neigbourhood WhatsApp group, and as we wander tentatively down the road, just a block away, the air is aswirl with red and blue lights and the cry of sirens.

In the glare of headlights and torches, we see the Land Cruiser, wedged between a tree and a wall, its airbags deflated, its tyres folded, a wisp of white smoke curling from the engine.

Slowly, in whispers and breathless fragments, the story is pieced together in the cluster on the opposite pavement.

There was a shooting at the pharmacy – inside the pharmacy? – no, outside the pharmacy, not a shooting, but a hijacking; some-one – a security guard? A civilian? – fired at the hijackers as they drove off, hitting both. The other car – what other car? An X5, it was a white BMW X5 – sped away from the scene, after the Land Cruiser crashed.

With each telling, the details shift, like the red-lit shadows on the high security walls, until, in the cold light of the day, comes the official version, in the form of a media statement from SAPS: 'The hijacking in progress was witnessed by an off-duty police officer

who was at the pharmacy. He then confronted the suspects by firing several shots. The suspects could not manage to drive far as
they crashed the hijacked vehicle into a tree. The driver died at the
scene and the other was injured. The injured suspect was taken to
the hospital under police guard. Police also seized two handguns
at the scene.'

This morning, I took a walk down the road again, and the car
was gone, and in its place, there was a scattering of plastic and
metal parts, shards, wiring, pipes, the guts of machinery.

The bark had been scraped from the tree on the pavement,
exposing the raw, yellow wood beneath. The earth had been stirred
up, and the trails of the tyres gave way to sprinklings of white powder from a spent fire extinguisher.

Here and there, a few pairs of discarded surgical gloves, and a
tinted window, crumpled like a fistful of paper.

In the distance, I could hear the rush of traffic on the freeway,
and closer to home, a dog barking, birds chirping, and the buzzing
of the bees on a mild Summer day in my suburb.

The meaning of swag

'Swag'. In Millen-nialese, the arcane dialect of the generational sub-tribe, it means, as far as I am independently able to ascertain (one doesn't put such questions directly to the source), a thing or situation of which one approves.

Examples thereof would be a pair of Vans or a Kendrick Lamar album (things), and a seat in the boat of the Old Saints Eight that triumphantly won their race at the regatta at Roodeplaat Dam on Saturday (situations).

Also swag, would be turning 21 and getting a home-baked cake to prove it, even if, upon seeing it, Max asked Rachel why the cake said 12 instead of 21. It's all a matter of perspective.

The first in this set of pictures shows Max expressing his impatience at my slow rate of picture-taking – 'You're LITERALLY taking forever to take a single picture! I OBVIOUSLY haven't got all day!' – and the second shows him feeling swag as he waits to have his cake and eat it too.

We have similar sets of images from over the years – Max has always been a little impatient when it comes to such protracted ceremonies as cutting the cake.

I am a little concerned about what Max's reaction might be when he sees these pictures, but then again, I don't think he uses Facebook much – it's not very swag.

As a Millennial respondent for my MA Journalism research project told me, when I enquired about his social media habits,

'Facebook is for old people, and Instagram is Twitter for people who can't read.'

Have a swag birthday, Max, and enjoy the Stella Artois – as a rower, rowing coach, B.Comm student, and all-round good oke, you've earned it!

The athletes of ballet, poised between pain and grace

I went to see a ballet today: *Giselle*, at the Joburg Theatre. I don't often get dragged along to the ballet, and when I do, I generally find it very hard to follow the plot, given that there is no dialogue or scrolling news bar like you get on CNN.

But we got there early to avoid the traffic, so I had some time, way up in the stalls, to look up the story of *Giselle* on Wikipedia, as the orchestra tuned up in the pit.

I always enjoy that free-form cacophony, the oboe snaking up and down its scales, the violins scraping away the dust, the French horn tooting and parping in French.

I had only a vague idea that *Giselle* is the one in which a doll comes to life, and dances on and on and on, but it turned out I was wrong about that.

Giselle is the one about the beautiful young peasant girl who falls for a deceitful nobleman, after which she dances on and on and on, until she dies of a broken heart. Then, in Act 2, she carries on dancing on and on, this time as a ghost. That's a lot of dancing.

I was pleased I had remembered the binoculars – or the opera glasses, as one calls them when they are deployed in a theatre – which allowed me to get a close-up view of the action onstage, the hairdo of the person in front of me notwithstanding.

Early in the first act, at the point where Giselle is dancing with a blissful smile on her face, at a market or a harvest festival (my phone was off, so I couldn't check) it struck me just how much ballet treads a fine line, en pointe, between pain and grace, between beauty and punishment, between artistry and athleticism.

Those flying leaps, those twirls, those lifts, those pirouettes, those spins, are performed to meticulous precision under the hot lights, and the dancers, all the while, must gesture and emote and tell a story, without words and without, as far as I could see, breaking a sweat.

The lightness of their footfalls, the fluidity of their movement, the sinew of their muscles: I was awestruck.

Because ballet is an art-form, we don't categorise it or see it as a sport, and yet, I was as much moved by the strength and endurance of the dancers today as I was by Eliud Kipchoge's deceptively easy striding towards the finish of his sub-two-hour marathon in Vienna yesterday.

Can a marathon be viewed as a form of creative expression? Can ballet be viewed as a form of athletic endeavour?

Either way, when the runner is garlanded with a bouquet, and the long-stemmed roses cascade onto the stage, it is the human spirit we are celebrating, honouring the way it puts our limits to the test and brings out the best in us, striding onward and onward like Kipchoge, or dancing on and on like Giselle.

When some sweet-talking song comes along

Pop music is made for the masses – that's why it's called pop – but the paradox of its popularity is that it is equally made for individuals, for you and I, for anyone who has ever felt the words and music of a song cutting through the crowd and arrowing straight to their heart and soul.

A good piece of pop will feel like a personal epistle, connecting us forever to a place and time and state of mind, and it will linger in the jukebox of memory, ready to be replayed at the slightest impulse or shift in the alignment of the planets.

Today, it was a headline in *The New York Times*: 'Daryl Dragon, of the Captain and Tennille Pop Duo, Dies at 76'.

Suddenly, I was in my matric art class all over again, painstakingly daubing oils on paper during a practical exam, with the radio playing in the background. Our art master, Mr Disbergen, if I recall correctly, thought it would help to ease us at our easels into the right creative frame, that transcendent state of Zen known as 'flow', where you are able to do a thing without thinking too much about the thing you are doing. And this was the song that was playing.

'Love Will Keep Us Together', by Captain & Tennille. There was something in that insistent, angular synth line, that trilling sweep of honky-tonk piano, that dreamy, silken swirl of Tennille's voice, that immediately lifted me up, and I have been in love with the song ever since, even though I haven't actively listened to it in years.

Today, hearing it on Spotify again, I sensed for the first time the darkness in its undercurrent, the tug of obsessive possessiveness that lends ambiguity to the simplest of lines: 'You better stop/ Don't mess around/You belong to me now/Ain't gonna set you free now'.

But that is the tension that underpins all the best pop songs, the counterpoint between the upbeat and the down, and it finds its perfect proof in the corollary to this seemingly sunny song: Joy Division's 1980 ballad, 'Love Will Tear Us Apart', which deconstructs a relationship on a palette of exquisite pain.

'Love Will Keep Us Together' came out of nowhere in 1975, going on to be a Number 1 hit on the Billboard singles chart, and Record of the Year at the Grammys.

But for me, it was the background music of my art class, the polar opposite of the hard rock and progressive jazz-fusion that defined my taste and attitude at the time, and while it played for just a couple of minutes on the radio, it felt like it was playing just for me, and that is why it will swirl around in my head all day, or at least until the next sweet-talking song comes along.

A signature evening with a literary idol

Years ago, in a previous century, on my first-ever visit to New York City, wandering around in a daze, dizzied by the sight of the starscrapers looming in the crisp night air, my tongue still burning from the swig of too-hot coffee I had foolishly taken at the Port Authority Terminal, I chanced upon the doorway of an ornate stone edifice on West 44th Street.

I stopped in my tracks, not because this building housed the Library of the General Society of Mechanics and Tradesmen of the City of New York, as it said on the plaque, but because there was a notice on the door that read: 'Champagne Fest, 6 pm, Featuring Tom Wolfe, Author. Price: $15 (Tax Deductible)'.

That was a lot of $$$ back in those days – I think it must have been the mid-1980s – but I didn't hesitate for a moment.

I opened the door, walked in, and there sat a lady who was getting ready to lock up her steel money box for the night. I asked her if I could have a ticket. 'He's almost finished, you know,' she said, dashing me a quizzical look, and I could hear a voice echoing a little further down.

That's fine, I said, and I handed her a green banknote, and she handed me some green banknotes back. She pointed down the carpeted hallway, and I wandered quietly along it and snuck into a lecture room with plush old chairs of pale wood and black leather, and I sat down at the back with a nod of apology.

Tom Wolfe, the author, was standing at the podium, wearing his trademark white suit with wide lapels, looking just like he looked on the back of the books I had read and re-read like gospel.

The Kandy-Kolored Tangerine-Flake Streamline Baby; The Electric Kool-Aid Acid Test; The Right Stuff; Radical Chic & Mau-Mauing the Flak Catchers; The New Journalism.

He must have been an hour or more into his talk, and I could see that he was wrapping up, and he wasn't talking about himself or his own work. He was talking about a French writer of the 19th century, Émile Zola, whose most famous work is a book called *Germinal*, a novel about a coalminers' strike in a small village in the far north of the country.

As part of his research for the book, Zola spent some time living in the village, getting to know the miners, their families, and the squalor of their working and living conditions.

One day, Zola went down the mine, and there, in the blackness, illuminated by the flickering lamps, he saw a white horse, a big, muscular creature whose job was to pull the coal-carts.

Zola was mesmerised by the sight of the animal, and puzzled by the logistics of getting such a hefty workhorse into and out of the mine every day. He asked one of the miners, who gave him a curious, uncomprehending stare.

'The horse lives down here,' he said. For 10 years, the horse had never seen the surface or the light of day. That image, of a beast of burden confined to the pit, became the central metaphor of Zola's book, and for Tom Wolfe, the journalist, a century later, it was a perfect example of the stories journalists must tell, and the meaning they must seek out and unlock amidst the suffocating chaos of the world. And there he ended his talk.

I sat there for a while, stunned, and then I thought, I've come all this way, I've paid $15, I can't leave without meeting the author and shaking his hand and saying a few quick words.

So I waited my turn, I took a deep breath, and I said – I remember, clearly, every word – 'Good evening, Mr Wolfe, do you know you have a very devoted following in South Africa?' He cocked his eyebrow: 'Oh, really?' 'Yes,' I said. 'Me.'

And then I asked him, like a wide-eyed fan, if he would mind signing an envelope in my Filofax (a kind of early analogue version of the smartphone, circa the 1980s), and he did, with a flourish and a smile, and I have treasured his autograph ever since.

Tom Wolfe, author, died today in New York at the age of 88. Rest in peace, Mr Wolfe, and thank you for your writing.

The man who went out of his way to say thank you for his coffee

I have just finished reading *Thanks A Thousand*, by the American author and journalist AJ Jacobs.

It is a book with a preposterous premise, one that begins when the author, fed up with being fed up, irritated by his own irritability, decides to embark on a journey to a different state of mind.

Over a shot of his favourite mood-altering narcotic – a coffee at Joe Coffee Company in Brooklyn, New York – he sets out to count his blessings, and more importantly, to bless those along the way who count.

As the caffeine takes effect, he realises with a jolt that he has come to take his daily fix for granted. No more.

'Thank you for my coffee,' he says to the barista, and thus begins his epic quest, a kind of coffee-fuelled Camino, to thank as many people as he can for the role they play in bringing him his brew.

The trail takes him all the way from the serving to the roasting to the sourcing to the shipping to the growing and harvesting of the miracle bean on a farm in the lowlands of Colombia, where, in a touching scene, he reads a scribbled note of gracias in his rudimentary Spanish to a family on the porch of their homestead.

In all, he thanks more than a thousand people (hence the title), ranging from the designer of the Joe Coffee Company logo, to a bunch of truckers in a warehouse, to a chemist in a lab at a massive water reservoir in upstate New York.

He even throws in a retrospective thank you to Kaldi the goatherd, the legendary Ethiopian who, several centuries ago, noticed his flock jumping with renewed vigour whenever they nibbled the bright red berries of a certain bush.

It's good to know that Africa gave the gift of coffee to the world, along with music, art, language, and, well, humanity. Indeed, the book is threaded through with an unspoken ideal that will be very familiar to all of us here on the southern edge: the notion that we are what we are, because of each other.

When we say thank you, in that spirit, we are using a word that is etymologically rooted to an ancient Indo-European word that means 'think'.

So to thank someone means that you are bound to them in thought and deed; you are connected, however fleetingly, by the act and its acknowledgement.

In this short and sweet book, the author plucks at these invisible threads that bind us, and the coffee becomes the symbol for a greater treatise on the meaning of gratitude in modern life.

Thankfully, that sweetness is leavened here and there by the author's cynical wit and self-doubt, because it is a little crazy, let's face it, to go around thanking total strangers for their homoeopathically diluted degree of contribution to your caffeine buzz.

But he perseveres, even when waved away by a factory worker who doesn't want to be thanked, or has the phone put down on him by a prospective thankee who suspects him of being a cold-call salesman.

AJ Jacobs has made his name as a journalist who takes a quirky idea and turns it into a reality-style social experiment: in *My Year of Living Biblically*, he grows a Moses-regulation beard and sets out to live his life by the strictest of Old Testament precepts; in *The Know-It-All*, he aims to become the smartest person on earth by obsessively reading all 32 volumes of the *Encyclopaedia Britannica*.

But this is my favourite of all his books, because it shifts the spotlight away from himself, and onto all of us.

So much of our daily discourse is taken up by sniping, for reasons both petty and grand, personal and universal – face-to-face or on the social networks.

Curmudgeonliness has its place in the world, and shared complaining, say in a Home Affairs queue, can be a healthy form of catharsis and ubuntu.

But how rarely do we stop, think, unravel the moment, and say: 'Thanks for this.' The power that comes from not taking something for granted, I learn anew from this book, should never be taken for granted.

I thank you for reading, and AJ Jacobs, I thank you for writing a book that shines a whole new light on two of the most important things in this world. Gratitude, and coffee.

Fire and rebirth

Scatterlings of charred wood, ghostly trails of ash, and the back-of-the-throat scratch of blackened veld crumbling underfoot, are all that remain of the long walkway to the Mankwe Hide, after a raging wildfire swept through vast tracts of the Pilanesberg National Park in the North West this week.

The hide, a favourite of birdwatchers, offered a panoramic view of the Mankwe Dam, with the branches of half-sunken trees reaching like fingers from the depths.

Here, cormorants perched and kingfishers swooped and fish eagles tore the silence with their lonely cry.

You could look down into the waters and see the terrapins stirring up the silt, and on the far banks, a crocodile lying in wait, as still as a statue made of bronze, or a herd of elephant lumbering out for a late-afternoon drink.

The veld is still Winter-dry and crisp on the cusp of Spring, and fire is the way nature cleanses and reinvents itself, season after season.

The hide may be gone, but the bush, in the open, carries on with its cycle, and as we stood and watched, a white speck in the distance lifted into the air and revealed itself, with a span of wings and a cry, to be a fish eagle, returning to its haunt after the flames had subsided and disappeared into the clouds.

Hobbits of the Civil Service

'**M**a'am, can you give me protection from yourself?' This astonishing response by Mmamathe Makhekhe-Mokhuane, chief officer of digital and IT at SARS, to a straightforward interview question about restructuring at the revenue authority, has been nagging me like a popcorn kernel in a tooth all week long.

It was such a strange thing to say, such a non sequitur, so unexpectedly defensive and passive aggressive, that the interviewer, Sakina Kamwendo of *Morning Live*, could only shake her head and giggle incredulously.

While Makhekhe-Mokhuane has since apologised to the nation for her 'conduct, posture, and demeanour' during the interview, that phrase will live long in infamy, or at least in training sessions on how not to deal with the media.

But what had really been bugging me was where I had heard the bell ringing before, and today I finally managed to figure it out.

It hails from a scene in the first instalment of the Lord of the Rings trilogy, where Aragorn, escort of the hobbits, the best swordsman in all of Middle-earth, confronts Frodo re the whereabouts of the ring.

'Stay away!' commands Frodo, whereupon Aragorn, advancing open-handed, says, 'Frodo! I swore to protect you.' To which the cloaked and curly-haired hobbit, his face a portrait of fear and anxiety, responds: 'Can you protect me from yourself?'

I suspect that JRR Tolkien, who of course was born in Bloemfontein, would have been very interested to hear this modern-day variant of that poignant line, repurposed as proof that some civil servants will never be able to get out of the hobbit of answering a question with a question.

The hard-headed meat-eater who wants to save the world from meat

Pleased to meet you, meat to please you, runs the old butchery slogan, and today it was my pleasure to meet a man whose work in the field may forever change the way we think about the meat we eat.

His name is Professor Mark Post, and he is a Dutch pharmacologist, a 'tissue engineer' and Professor of Vascular Physiology at Maastricht University.

He is also the world's leading expert on the act of organic alchemy by which cultivated cells from live animals are transformed under laboratory conditions into, well, meat.

The process is known as cellular agriculture, and it has massive implications for food security, farming, and our ancient relationship with the beasts of the field, the once-wild herds whose domestication some 10 000 years ago served as one of the cornerstones of human civilisation.

We've come a long way since then, and the big question is not only whether it is humane and civilised for us to continue farming cattle in the way that we do, but whether it is economically and environmentally sustainable.

As the prof pointed out in his presentation at the SingularityU South Africa Summit in Kyalami, cattle-farming is a singularly inefficient business: 'We're already using 70 per cent of arable land for raising meat, and our consumption is expected to rise by 70 per cent. The maths doesn't work.'

There are currently approximately one-and-a-half billion head of cattle in the world, and I asked Professor Post how many we would need for the large-scale production of lab-cultured meat, which involves the extraction of stem cells from the muscle tissue of a cow.

'Oh, a couple of hundred,' he said, and I was wondering whether he meant thousand or million, but no, he meant a couple of hundred. 'You could feed the whole of Johannesburg with maybe one or two cows,' he added.

But as much as meat grown in a petri dish may be good for the environment, food security, and cattle themselves – laboratory-cultured meat is also known as 'slaughter-free meat' – the carnivores among us will still want to know: yes, but does it taste like meat?

To which the prof gives a wry smile and admits, in his soft Dutch accent, 'It's not great yet, but it's getting there. The first version we made was without fat, and that makes it a little dry and not as tasty. So we're now also making fat tissue, also from cow cells. We're gradually getting closer.'

The first cultured beef burger was presented to the press in London five years ago, and a food scientist who sampled it declared the patty to be 'crunchy and hot, a bit like cake.' The Marie Antoinette burger, then.

But with the rapid pace of development in the field, Professor Post expects meat-tasty meat from the labs to be commercially available within the next three years, assuming economies of scale and regulatory approval.

I asked the prof whether he expected cultural attitudes towards meat to be a barrier to the acceptance of the petri-dish variety, and he conceded that 'It's sort of ingrained in our minds that meat is a masculine thing, with the barbecue, fire, cowboys, hunting, supremacy over another species … and of course all that will change if you start to make it in a factory.'

Then again, remember, people happily eat hot dogs, without

necessarily knowing or wanting to know where they come from and how they are processed.

Professor Post himself is a 'hard-headed meat-eater', whose motives as a meat-culturer are primarily based on food security and the need to safeguard the integrity of the natural environment.

As a non-meat-eater myself, I wondered aloud whether vegans and vegetarians were likely to consume a product that is, at least at the cellular level, animal-based.

'For me, it's quite logical,' the prof answered. 'I usually tell vegans and vegetarians to not eat this, because what they are doing is refraining from animal proteins altogether, which is already much better for food security and the environment than I can do with cultured meat.'

Either way, food for thought, now and in the future.

Sprinkling Wildblumen over Weimar

The best book on writing that I have ever read is called *On Writing Well*. It is by the late William Zinsser, an American journalist, critic, and educator.

Aimed primarily at writers of non-fiction, the book is full of sage and useful advice, none of which I can recall right now, other than a single nugget that I am happy to share with you today. I call it The Principle of the One Thing.

Zinsser believes that in order for a piece of writing to succeed, it must leave the reader with one provocative thought, image, or idea that will linger in their memory and imagination. 'Not two thoughts, or five,' writes Zinsser, 'just one.'

On the face of it, this seems oddly counter-intuitive. Wouldn't you, as a writer, want your reader to absorb and remember everything you write? That would be nice, but it is not how reading works.

When we read, we intuitively filter what we need to know from what we don't. In this sense, reading is the same as all the other senses; it is a process of processing data, which we do selectively, in order to avoid the overwhelm of too much information.

The 'one thing', therefore, will be the thing that leaps from the page and stays with you, serving as an anchor, a bookmark, a placeholder that stands in for the whole. Let me give you an example.

I must have read JD Salinger's *The Catcher in the Rye* at least a dozen times over the years, but the one thing I remember, at the expense of everything else in the book, is the part where Holden Caulfield wonders where the ducks in the pond in Central Park go when the pond ices over in the Winter.

This is such a crucial scene in the story, a symbol of the teen-age Holden's quest for meaning in the chaos of an ever-changing world, that it acts as the nucleus for everything else that revolves around it.

Likewise, from all my years of acquaintance with *Slaughterhouse-Five*, by Kurt Vonnegut, the one image that sticks with me is the bombs floating serenely upwards into the bomb-bay over Dresden, a poignant reminder of destruction, regret, and the impossibility of turning time backwards.

Every book that is worth remembering and re-reading will have its One Thing, that in the end will become the entirety of what the book is about.

The reason I am telling you this is that I have just finished read-ing a very interesting book, a social history of an asocial condition: shyness in human beings. The book is *Shrinking Violets*, by Joe Moran.

It is a fascinating work, wittily told, woven through with illu-minating case-studies of the chronically shy, from Alan Turing to Agatha Christie to Morrissey.

But the one lingering thing I draw from the book is a short anec-dote about the German poet and author, Johann Wolfgang von Goethe, who was the brooding spearhead of the Sturm und Drang literary movement, and whose most famous work, *Faust*, is about a man who sells his soul to the devil.

There was another side to Goethe, however, and it is brought to light in this single line from Moran's book: 'Goethe used to carry violet seeds in his pockets, scattering them on his walks around Weimar as his own contribution to the beauty of the world.'

What a revelation this is. The image of the austere Goethe sprinkling Wildblumen over Weimar is, on the one hand, sweetly romantic; on the other, it is purely pragmatic, since he was a botanist too, and so he may just have been doing his duty.

But as with all such images, there is a deeper symbolism at the heart of it. Words and deeds are seeds, and the way we sow them can make the forest bloom, or can strangle its blossoms at the roots.

Gather ye rosebuds while ye may, advised the English poet Robert Herrick in the 17th century, but how much better a place would the world be if, in the manner of Goethe, we scattered violets all over it instead. And that, if I may, is the One Thing I will leave you with today.

True confessions of an X-phile

We're having a municipal by-election in my ward in Joburg soon, and today I got my first call from a canvasser for one of the competing parties. Not just any canvasser, but a senior member of the party, whose name I instantly recognised from his frequent mentions in dispatches.

We had a good chat, about the state of the ward, the state of the city, the state of the nation, the state of the parties. I was walking my dog in the park at the time, so I had a few minutes while she ran off the leash, even though, technically, letting a dog off the leash is in contravention of the bylaws of the very city in whose ward I'll be voting. Ah, well.

Then my canvasser asked me if he could count on my vote, and I said, sure, I'm definitely going to think about it, which is what I always say to canvassers from any political party.

It's not that I'm hedging my bets, it's just that, who knows, between now and Wednesday next week, what any particular party or candidate will do or say to make me change my mind.

I also like that moment when you're standing in the booth, and your pencil is hovering over the little empty boxes, and you're thinking to yourself, I could change the outcome of this whole election just by putting my X either here or there.

And then you put your X either here or there, and a little jolt of power surges through you: you've cast your vote, and whatever happens next, you will in some small way be able to take the credit or the blame. Usually, the way things turn out once people get elected, it'll be the blame, but either way, I do like elections.

The posters, the slogans, the hustling, the hustings, the promises, the put-downs, the propaganda. Especially, the propaganda. A small election in a municipal ward offers a highly concentrated opportunity to win hearts and minds, and I have no objection at all to any attempt to win me over, whether it's in the form of an SMS or an email or a pamphlet or a cold call from a canvasser.

Political parties and independent candidates have every right to reach out to voters, using any platform and technology at their disposal, and more than that, they have a duty: how else will we be able to learn what they stand for, and to give them a chance to put their powers of rhetoric and persuasion to the test?

The scattershot SMS is probably the least effective tool, because they come and go in a blip, and you can delete them without reading, which is what I do all the time with SMSes from my bank.

The most effective would be the house-to-house call from the candidate, but that rarely happens these days, in part because it's so hard to find a house in the suburbs of Johannesburg with a working gate-buzzer.

But hey, if you've got something to say, and you're standing in my ward, and I can hear you hooting over the barking of the dogs, I'll happily invite you in for tea and a talk, and I'll definitely think about giving you my vote, because that, after all, is what democracy is all about. Tea, and promises.

No such thing as a free coffee

'Free Coffee', said the sign that caught my eye as we strolled along the promenade in Umhlanga, and I wondered whether there would be another catch. There was.

The coffee was free, all right, but the T & C that applied was: 'if you collect a bucket of litter off the beach'.

That sounded to me like a fair trade for a flat white, so I stood in the queue at the little kiosk of the Rox Coffee Company, and as everyone else ordered their espresso and Americano and macchiato and golden latte (with almond milk, turmeric, black pepper, cinnamon, coconut oil, and honey), I, when I got to the front, ordered a bucket.

As the barista reached under the counter and handed it over, my heart sank. It was a big bucket.

Earlier, as we ambled along the snaking walkway between the candy-striped lighthouse and the whale rib-cage pier, I had remarked on the spotlessness of the precinct – there literally wasn't a speck of litter to be seen, despite the hordes of holidaymakers, teen-ragers, and Umhlangaterians in town.

I set off, my bucket swinging slowly to and fro in my hand, my eyes on the litterless path, with its beckoning swirl of red-and-brown Corobrik. To make matters worse, I was alone in my quest.

Amanda was quickening her pace, increasing the distance between herself and my obsession. 'Most people who come to Umhlanga get taken to the Oyster Box for high tea,' she said, as I stooped to pick up a stompie – yay, a stompie! – from the edge of the kerb. 'Me, I get to walk with someone filling a bucket with trash in the hope of exchanging it for a free coffee.'

But by the time I reached the fringes of the lush and tangled Hawaan Forest, which I bypassed for the wooden stairway leading to the beach, the tide was beginning to turn.

As an inlander, whenever I walk on the beach, I am lulled into a state of Zen contemplation by the roar and shhh of the waves.

I think about the big questions: how many grains of sand on the shore? How many scatterlings of light upon the breakers? Does the tiny fish, flitting in the rockpool, perceive the rockpool to be the entirety of the ocean? But now, all I was thinking was, where is all the rubbish.

I grew more expert as I walked along, learning to tell the difference between a cuttlefish bone and a polystyrene cup, a ready-to-pop bluebottle and a deflated plastic bag, the sheen of a wave-washed pebble and ... ah, a beer-bottle.

I kneed my way up the dune, grabbing onto a tree-root for leverage, and I pulled the shell of a Heineken from its harbour. It was clogged with thick, dark sand. I tapped it against the tree, and the sand blew away.

I put the bottle in the bucket, and then another, and another. I reached for a tin, stripped of its branding by the winds of time. It crumpled into flakes of rust in my hand. I walked along. An empty box of Hookies sardine-bait. A Lay's crisp-packet. A yoghurt tub. The clam-shell of a takeaway burger box. A Winston cigarette carton.

It struck me, as I looked to the sea, that we evolved, if you accept the scientific hypothesis, from enzymes that spawned from the deep, and that the first evidence of our being, as you work your way towards the shore, is the garbage we leave behind. What is archaeology, after all, other than the practice of sifting through other people's trash?

At the lagoon, with its coffee-coloured ripples, cleaved at low tide from the ocean, I up-ended my haul and took stock of my bucket-list. Surely by now I had enough for the coffee I was craving. But it was hard to kick the habit.

I saw something pink and plastic, half-embedded in the sand, and I was about to pick it up, when a dad glared at me from underneath his umbrella. I realised I was looking at a toy beach-spade, in the shape of a shell. I let it be.

I stopped to make my acquaintance with an Akita pup, a big, fluffy breed of dog from Japan, and its walking companion, spying my bucket, said, 'Oh, well done,' and then, with a sigh: 'Aren't humans trashy?' I didn't have the nerve to tell her that my environmental activism was incentivised by caffeine.

As I climbed the stairs back to the promenade, a man ran up to me, waved, and handed me an empty Brutal Fruit bottle. 'Thanks, hey!' he said. My bucket was full and clinking.

At the kiosk of the Rox Coffee Company, I showed it to the barista, and he nodded amidst the hissing of steam.

The concept of trash for cash, I should add, is not all that new: in various parts of the developing world, including India and South Africa, there are programmes in place to encourage communities to gather and swap garbage for WiFi, school supplies, and basic commodities.

But I hadn't heard of trash for coffee before. My flat white, let me tell you, was good. But nowhere near as good as the feeling I got when I crumpled up the cup and threw it in the bin, where all the garbage we generate and leave behind, rightfully belongs.

Once upon a Star

Today I had a meeting at *The Star*, the last of the big city newspapers left in the big city of Johannesburg. It's at 47 Pixley ka Isaka Seme Street, formerly 47 Sauer Street, and it's directly opposite Luthuli House, the national headquarters of the ANC.

The two buildings are so close, that you could probably lean out of a window of *The Star* and yell at a spokesperson for comment on a developing story, or conversely, lean out of a window of Luthuli House and randomly yell at a journalist.

Next to Luthuli House is an empty lot where once stood the Elizabeth Hotel, in whose pub many a journalist once stood and fell, and yet miraculously managed to make it back to the newsroom in time to bash out a story for the next edition.

The Star itself is housed in a building of many storeys, all of them drab and unlovely, as if the hard-scrabble industry of journalism leaves no time for niceties and flourishes.

This heroic mural in the lobby, of a newspaper being perused, steaming hot off the press, is as decorative as it gets. And yet, when I worked at *The Star*, as a junior reporter, I thought this was the most exciting building on the face of the earth.

To walk into the newsroom on the first floor was to feel a pulse-quickening surge of adrenaline, a physical sensation that was compounded by the clattering of typewriters, the ringing of telephones, the shouting of battle-commands over the din, and the earthquake-rumble of the printing presses somewhere deep in the Dickensian basement, where no mere reporter would ever dare to tread.

I remember so well my first day at *The Star*. It was my big city break, as a junior hack whose only previous experience was in the tiny newsroom of the *West Rand Times* in Krugersdorp.

I arrived bright and early, or at least early, on my first day, only to discover that the entire building was shrouded in an eerie, post-apocalyptic silence, with no human to be seen, save for a sleepy-eyed security guard, who eyed me with a mixture of pity and bemusement.

It was New Year's Day, and I had naïvely thought that my work would begin, as per contract, on that traditional day off. The guard advised me to report for duty on a less-hungover day, which I duly did.

I greatly enjoyed my spell at *The Star*, rushing off to stories with Nikon-slinging, chain-smoking photographers who drove like demons and barged in with their trigger-fingers firing, while I scoured the scene for a telephone-booth from which I could call the dictate desk and file my hastily scrawled copy.

After a couple of months of this, the news ed called me into his office one day and told me, given my vast experience in the area, that I was being transferred to the West Rand bureau of *The Star*, which was based in Krugersdorp.

It was good to be back at HQ for the first time in decades today, and to be reminded that whatever else may change in the world of modern media, a big city without a big city newspaper at its heart and soul, is just a big city.

The Year of the Three Revolutions

AT LAST.
A CELLULAR
PHONE
THAT WON'T
CUT OUT
IN THE
MIDDLE OF

Every time Freedom Day rolls around, I am reminded that 1994, in South Africa, was The Year of the Three Revolutions.

Firstly, of course, there were the long, snaking lines, busy with chatter and the buzz of expectation, the sense in the mellow Autumn air of being part of something big and important and earth-changing, and yet, when you finally got to the front, something as simple and fleeting as drawing two intersecting diagonal lines on a piece of paper and slipping it into a slot.

Then, out of the deep, wide blue, came a strange, invisible force of nature that would mutate into an omnipresent force of humanity.

I can't recall exactly where I was, in 1994, when I first overheard somebody talking about 'The Internet' – a noisy newsroom, perhaps? – but I do recall the frisson I felt at the time.

It sounded to me like something malevolent and Orwellian, and it was only when I sat down in front of a computer, with the Netscape browser opening sesame to the World Wide Web, that I realised it was a force born out of hope rather than fear, and that it had come to change the world for the good.

I still haven't changed my mind on that, despite what people sometimes have to say to each other on the internet.

And then there was the Third Revolution, which was really more of an evolution: the telephone, set free at last from its tethers.

The big sell with the cellular telephone, which arrived in March

1994, its commercial launch brought forward to accommodate the needs of election monitors in the field, was that you could 'reach the person, and not the place'.

I remember standing in another queue, at a department store in a mall in Randburg, to sign up for my very own cellphone, which was available, to paraphrase Henry Ford's famous line, in any model you wanted, as long as it was a Nokia 1011.

A hefty beast of a brick, with a tiny rectangular screen, and a button-pull antenna that reached for the skies. And all you could do with it was talk to people on it, and that was more than enough.

Within just a few months, the first cellphone had spawned a host of other cellphones, and by the middle of 1994, the state-of-the-tech was this much more compact Ericsson, the GH 198, seen here in a double-page spread in *Style* magazine, its three-and-a-half-hour talktime being trumpeted above all else, because, well, there was nothing else it had.

It would be another 13 years before Steve Jobs held the first iPhone in his hand, and raised it in the air in triumph, and the world shifted anew on its axis.

It's odd that we still call these things phones, out of sheer force of habit and want of a better option, when the least amazing thing they can do is phone, and when the sight of someone talking on a phone, rather than simply staring down at it, is almost as curious today as it was back then.

A six-year-old child could have drawn this logo JOLENE

Jolene, aside from being the name of Dolly Parton's most famous song, is also the name of a trendy bakery and restaurant in north London.

The Guardian, in a rhapsodic review, described the cuisine as 'earthy, imaginative, slightly saintly, but with a dirty underbelly of oily, salty largesse'.

That sounds delicious, and definitely makes Jolene worthy of a place on your to-eat list for your next visit to the UK capital.

In the meantime, feast your eyes on the restaurant's new logo, happily at home amidst the décor of unplastered walls and stainless-steel tables.

The restaurant's brief to the design studio was to come up with a logo that was 'naïve, almost childish', to reflect the ethos of sustainable farming in the interest of future generations.

In a bold and daring stroke of genius, the owner of the studio, Frith Kerr, outsourced the design to a young freelancer who had never worked on a commercial project before: her six-year-old son, Igor.

She asked him to write the restaurant's name in his own style, after which she selected the final logotype from a variety of options.

She then presented the design to the restaurant, with all due credit to the designer, highlighting 'the inimitable spacing and crescendo of elegant sans-serif capital letterforms'.

The logotype's handmade nature, added Frith, gave it the potential to 'exist in many forms without it feeling out of place with the space, whether it's embroidered on a window curtain or stamped loosely on a menu'.

The client loved it, and so do I, in part because it reminds me of Picasso's famous saying: 'It took me four years to paint like Raphael, but a lifetime to paint like a child.'

Cast your mind back to when you were six years old. Remember how it felt to pick up a pencil, or to choose a wax crayon from that rainbow of sweet-smelling colours, and to write or draw without fear, without hesitation, without worrying about what others would think or say.

The joy and freedom of unhindered, unleashed creativity in its purest, most primal form. That is what this logo represents: the radical naivety of childhood.

I have in my home a painting by the late South African pop artist Paul du Toit, who signed his work in capital letters, with a backwards-facing L.

A friend once visited us, saw the painting from afar, and said, 'Oh, did Max paint that? It's lovely!' Max, at the time, was four years old.

I later told Paul of this reaction to his work, and he smiled and said it was the greatest compliment an artist could ever receive: that he saw the world through the eyes of a child, and tried to paint it that way.

Bringing home the beacon

One of the things I like most about Facebook, versus Twitter, is that you can go back and edit your posts, which is a very generous concession to human fallibility and the high odds of finger-slippage.

Just one letter missed in the typerush can completely alter the meaning of a tweet that may otherwise have been overlooked or forgotten in the stream.

Twitter doesn't yet allow editing of tweets for any reason; the best you can do is delete the tweet and repost, which is a schlepp of epic proportions and also, really, a complete waste of time, because once tweeted and seen, even for a nanosecond, it's already too late to fix. So you may as well leave it be.

Here is my favourite Freudian Twitslip of the week, from the United Nations, proving once again that if you're going to make a rasher decision and misspell a word on Twitter, you may as well go the whole hog.

You've got an Uncle Pravin in the furniture business

Pravin Gordhan, the hitherto conspicuously un-nicknamed Minister of Public Enterprises, has finally joined the serried ranks of South African politicians with amusing nicknames.

He is now known, at least to the battalions of EFF fighters who have dubbed him thusly in their tweets, as Joshua Doore, on account of his uncanny resemblance to the benevolent hair-winged mascot of the furniture store of that name, and also because of his assumed avuncular relationship to the forces of, you know, the neoliberal capitalist conspiracy that really runs the country.

While such allegations remain as yet un-Pravin, the barrage of Twitter missiles launched against the Minister stem from his admission that he did, despite earlier denials, meet with at least one Gupta at some point when the Guptas were really running the country.

This was enough for Floyd Shivambu, the EFF's Deputy Commander-in-Tweet, to accuse Gordhan of being 'the mob's uncle', without explicitly spelling out who the mob were.

Curiously, while the merest mention of Joshua Doore will bring that catchy jingle – 'You've got an uncle in the furniture business' – to mind for millions of South Africans, there never really was a Joshua Doore, just as there never really was, sorry to say, a Clement Mugg and Joshua Fenomah Bean.

Indeed, the history of the fictional Joshua Doore goes back

to the early 1970s, when Harvey Leach, a retail entrepreneur in Detroit, Michigan, USA, took over a small store named Robinson Furniture, and changed its name to Joshua Doore.

The accompanying ad slogan for his newly christened store was an immediate hit in its jingle form, as it was when the brand arrived in South Africa in the same decade.

Joshua Doore stores, once ubiquitous, no longer exist on our shores, although the JD Group that bought the company has grown into a blue-chip giant, with Russells, Bradlows, Rochester, Sleepmaster, HiFi Corp, and Incredible Connection in its portfolio.

But there is a grisly footnote, sad to say, to the story of Joshua Doore, and it takes us right into the ganglands of Southfield, Detroit, where the body of Harvey Leach, the founder of the company, was found in the trunk of his Cadillac, one day in 1974.

His murder, widely believed to be a mob hit, remains unsolved, and Joshua Doore, the brand and the company, have long disappeared into the mists of memory.

To a generation of South Africans, Joshua Doore will always be the uncle we all had in the furniture business, even if, in the sound and fury of our political theatre, he will now henceforth forever be associated with a Cabinet Minister who looks uncannily like him.

Autumn, you are Winter's enabler

This morning I noticed that a leaf on the bonsai acacia tree in my study had turned overnight from a deep and lustrous green to the yellow of faded parchment.

I leaned in for a closer look – I had somehow thought the bonsai would be evergreen – and the leaf trembled at my breath, and then slowly, twirlingly, it fell to the bed of grit and gravel below.

Thus does Autumn arrive on the Highveld, with a subtle shift in the air, a stillness you can hear, a mellowing of the light that paints the sky in watery smudges of grey.

The seasons blur into one another here – there are no sharp lines that set them apart – and Autumn, the buffer, the interval, the pause for contemplation, lasts only a few short weeks, as the days compress, the evenings turn crisp, and the trees try on their new Fall range.

This is my favourite season in Johannesburg, suspended, like a falling leaf, between the righteous fury of the electric Summer storms and the sudden, shocking bite of Winter as it drifts in from the snowy mountains in the Berg.

A few years ago, I ran a writing workshop in Cape Town, at around this time of the season. The mountain stood purple against the fleecy sky, and I braced myself against the horizontal rain as I walked past the canals on Adderley Street.

Upstairs, I asked the class to try some free-writing – just put your head down and write for 20 minutes or so, without thinking too much about it – on the subject of: Autumn.

Most treated it with a lyrical reverence, but there was one writer who penned a vivid, livid rant against the season, berating it for its sullen indecisiveness and its bouts of bitter, drizzly cold. 'Autumn,' she concluded, 'you are Winter's enabler.' That line has stayed with me.

On the Highveld, Autumn is a time of burnished in-betweens, of crystal-blue, cloudless skies, of lazy, benevolent sunshine. Here, Autumn is Winter's denier.

It holds back the icy onslaught like an army in a fort, until, one day, when you least expect it, Winter marches in and boots the season into memory, and the trees, shed of their leaves, stand bare. Welcome, Autumn, once again. To every season there is a time, and yours is here and now.

The joy of ambient zhoozsh

I am stoked to see, via an article in *Slate* today, that the famous South African slang term 'zhoozsh' is fast becoming a famous international slang term.

We'll forgive the variance in spelling, since words often shift their shape in transition across the waters, and zhoozsh itself is a variant of its original usage, which was 'Jewish', as a synonym for stylish and fashionable.

The etymology of zhoozsh dates back to Joburg in the 1960s, when it was originally styled in Isicamtho as 'iJuwish', in reference to the perceived stylishness of snappy Jewish dressers in the city, and also to the predominance of Jewish tailors in the downtown clothing trade.

According to the master text on Seffrican English, *A Dictionary of South African English on Historical Principles* (Oxford University Press), iJuwish or Jewish thus came to mean 'Excellent, "cool", well-dressed, elegantly dressed'.

There is a reference from *Blame Me on History*, by Bloke Modisane, the celebrated Bard of old Sophiatown: 'The boys were expensively dressed in a stunning ensemble of colour, "Jewished", in their phraseology.'

And also this, from a 1973 fashion article in *Drum*: 'Maybe they were jealous of our expensive jewish. We pay for the clothes because we can afford them.'

By the 1980s, the arbiter of Highveld style and glam, *Style* magazine, was widely using the zhoozsh variant of Jewish, and the broadcaster Jeremy Mansfield later adopted it as his trademark, using it as the title of a cookbook co-authored with his wife, Jacqui.

Now zhoozsh has been all zhuzhed up for the global slang-market, thanks in part to its frequent usage by Carson Kressley, the fashion guru from the highly successful TV reality show, *Queer Eye for the Straight Guy*, now rebooted on Netflix as *Queer Eye*.

He happily uses zhuzh as a verb, as in, 'So many women were coming up to me asking, "How do I look?" or "Can you just zhuzh me?"'

And in a review of the show in *The New Yorker*, Troy Patterson speaks of the quality of 'ambient zhuzh', which will no doubt soon be in the lexicon of every on-trend interior designer or real estate agent.

Thus does zhuzh proudly join such now well-known South Africanisms as trek, kop, fundi, aardvark, Charlize Theron and ubuntu on the international stage. Have a lekker zhuzh day, hey.

One small step on a lunar sea

'Hey, Siri,' I enquired this week, holding my Apple Watch close to my lips, like an undercover agent checking in with base, 'what phase of the moon are we in tonight?'

The moon is full, she replied, in that silky-smooth voice that is too human to be human, with no edge of irritation or sigh of sarcasm, no matter how often I ask the same questions or issue the same commands.

So that evening, I looked up at the moon, the great glowing ghost-rock that beckons and seduces us, that sways our moods, that shifts the tides, that marks the coming and going of the months, that transforms us into lovers or werewolves under the light.

The shimmering halo shook as I zoomed in, through the binocs, on the dark patch of Mare Tranquillitatis, the Sea of Tranquillity, where 50 years ago the Eagle landed and Neil Armstrong took his backward jump-step off the ladder.

In that moment, the modern world was born, and still today we feel the aftershock, not just in the tremors and waves of technological progress, but in the deeply rooted sense that this remains humanity's most towering achievement, the off-earth landmark, in the lunar sea that bears the imprint of our arrival.

To look into the night sky is to dizzy yourself among the spinning of the stars, and no matter how quickly you may find an anchor in Crux, Orion, Venus, Jupiter, or Mars, when you see the moon, you will see a reflection of home. Because we've been there.

This week, in between talking to Siri and looking up, I watched *Apollo 11*, the brilliant new documentary about the first moon landing, and right from the opening shot, of the gargantuan Saturn

V rocket being ferried on a caterpillar-tread flatbed to the launch-pad, I was struck anew by the scale of the mission, by the crazy ambition that took a small step and turned it into a giant leap.

The Apollo astronauts, Armstrong, Aldrin, and Collins, ventured into the realm where only gods are meant to go, and it is no coincidence that their mission took its name from the god of truth and light, the patron of seafarers, the archer with the unfailing aim.

But that was Greek mythology; Apollo 11 was cold, hard mathematics, given shape and momentum in the belly of the machine.

I can't think, off-hand, of a more heart-stopping sequence in the history of the movies, captured with the Kodachrome clarity of newfound footage, than T minus 10 seconds and counting, when the engines ignite and a roaring plume of fire explodes from the base of the rocket, steering it straight as an arrow into the blue.

In that spark of uplift, everything fuses as one: the discovery of fire as a form of combustion, the invention of mechanised transport and communication across distance, the meeting of minds and sciences and technologies, the building of structures with heavenly aspirations, the spirit of quest and adventure that dares us to breach the horizon.

Apollo 11 was a bridge between worlds, humanity's long-shot at redemption. And that is why, exactly half a century after Neil Armstrong set foot on the powdery surface, we can look back at this crossing of the divide between history and the future, when the world held its breath, and the moon, for a moment, in all its fullness, held our dreams.

Lessons from a kumquat

This dimple-armoured pellet of juicy fruitiness, about the size of an olive, is technically known as a kumquat.

It is a member of the citrus family – a cousin, perhaps, or maybe a nephew – and it is often mistakenly referred to as a baby orange.

I brought a batch along with me to a creative writing workshop that I ran for high school students from Alexandra in Joburg this week.

They were attending a holiday camp at the premises of the Alexandra Education Committee, an NGO that provides bursaries and tuition for academically promising scholars.

The theme of the workshop was 'Writing with the Senses', the idea being that the way we perceive the world – through sight, touch, hearing, taste, and smell – can be a way to add vigour and life to your writing.

For instance, how would you describe the taste of a kumquat, to someone who has never tasted one before? Well, firstly, you have to taste one for yourself.

'Anyone know what this is?' I asked, holding up a kumquat. It's a litchi, said someone at the back of the class. A kiwi, said someone else. From upfront, getting closer: 'A baby orange.'

With a flourish of cursive, I skated the magic marker across the whiteboard, embarrassingly misspelling kumquat as 'kumqat', although, in my defence, it is just a mutually agreed transliteration of the Chinese name for the fruit.

Then I distributed the kumquats. Have a good look, I said. Touch it, feel it, smell it, taste it, write a few words about it. As the class would soon learn, the kumquat is the stealth missile of the citrus family.

It looks and smells orangey, not lemony, so you expect it to greet you with a rush of sweetness when you bite into it; instead, it erupts with a sudden astringency, a tart sting that makes your eyes water, and then the second wave of flavour charges through, and hey, it turns out to be sort of sweet after all, even as you eat every last shred of the peel. You can do that with a kumquat.

'I dig my teeth into the sweet-looking flesh,' wrote one of the students, 'and it reveals a bitter surprise.'

We compared notes, and almost everyone in the class had jotted down some thoughts about the benign appearance of the fruit, versus its seemingly malicious interior.

'It attacks you with its taste,' wrote another student, and this led to a discussion about perceptions and reality, and the kumquat, as we spoke, transformed itself from a citrus fruit into a metaphor for human relationships.

'Some people seem to be sweet when you first meet them, and then when you get to know them better, they turn out to be full of bitterness.'

Then again, the opposite may also prove to be true: isn't life, in its multitude of experiences and sensations, a bittersweet thing, rather than just one thing or the other? The neural networks of the brain are searching always, impulsively and subconsciously, for connections, leaps of logic, hidden meanings, symbols and metaphors.

This is the very basis of art, literature, poetry, music: we see, hear, touch, taste, smell one thing, and it makes us think of another. A rose is never just a rose; a kumquat is never just a kumquat.

And this week, as I watched a few brave souls venturing forth to pluck a second one from the tray, I realised once again how the senses we use to perceive the world can be the first small steps on the journey towards an epiphany.

Our tjatjarag nation

A charming tjatjaragness infuses our media and remains its distinguishing characteristic.

Journalism
Journalism
Journalism
Review 35

As seen on a poster of a pull-quote at the School of Journalism and Media Studies at Rhodes University, there are few words that sum up the flavour and tone of everyday South African sociopolitical discourse as tellingly as the tongue-tappingly percussive 'tjatjarag'.

It means, well, tjatjarag, there being no direct translation and no formal dictionary definition, although the crowdsourced online Urban Dictionary hazards the following: 'To be over-eager and excitable in an annoying manner.'

I would add cocky and impertinent to that list, since the most famous usage of tjatjarag occurred when Julius Malema, then President of the ANC Youth League, booted the BBC's Jonah Fisher out of a press conference at Luthuli House in 2010, for daring to question Malema's revolutionary credentials.

'You are tjatjarag!' huffed Malema, tjatjaragly, and the word instantly gained currency as an all-purpose insult or an ironic term of affection.

Tjatjarag is what you are when you talk back to a traffic cop, or ignore the repeated injunctions of the Speaker of the House; it is also what you are, oddly enough, if you are a traffic cop or a Speaker of the House, just trying, sighingly, to do your job above the hubbub.

So it is all really a matter of perspective, and we call each other tjatjarag as a general acknowledgement that to be a South African is to be, to all intents and purposes, ungovernable.

Here the national characteristic is even flattered as something charming, styled in its Anglicised form as 'tjatjaragness', when the more conventional form would be tjatjaragheid.

Tjatjarag seems to be a potjiekos word, with origins in the multilingual, criss-crossing borrowings and inventions of Isicamtho or Vlaaitaal.

But the precise etymology remains elusive, and I have yet to see an earlier documented usage than Malema's. Even the heftily authoritative *Dictionary of South African English on Historical Principles*, a project of The Dictionary Unit for South African English (DSAE), affiliated to Rhodes, does not contain an entry for the term.

Until the mystery is solved, say it loud, say it proud, and say it often, not necessarily because you find yourself in the presence of someone who is being over-eager and excitable in an annoying manner, but just sommer because you like the way it sounds. Tjatjarag.

Leonardo, Master of the Great Unfinished

L eonardo da Vinci, the original Renaissance Human, was famous for many things, among them the things he never got around to doing.

He never did finish the *Mona Lisa*, for instance, despite spending 16 years working on it, which is why it remains the best-known unsigned painting in the history of art.

And while working on another mega-masterpiece, *The Last Supper*, at the monastery of Santa Maria delle Grazie in Milan, he fell so far behind schedule that a prior at the monastery haughtily complained that the painter was taking too much time.

In response, Leonardo threatened to use the prior's face as the model for Judas in his fresco. The prior shut up.

Biographies of Leonardo, including the excellent *Da Vinci's Ghost*, by Toby Lester, which I am currently reading, paint him as a procrastinator of note, so much so that he makes all other crastinators look like mere amateurs.

Leonardo's big secret, or his big flaw, if you prefer, was that he was incredibly easily distracted, and prone to thinking and wondering too much about almost anything other than the job he was supposed to be doing.

Leonardo once drew an annotated to-do that serves as a fine example thereof. It reveals Leonardo reminding himself to embark on multiple journeys of learning and discovery, among them:

'Calculate the measurement of Milan and Suburbs; Get the master of arithmetic to show you how to square a triangle; Find out by what means they go on ice in Flanders; Ask Maestro Antonio how mortars are positioned on bastions by day or night; and Find a master of hydraulics and get him to tell you how to repair a lock, canal and mill in the Lombard manner.'

Leonardo carried a small notebook around with him, wherever he wandered, and as Lester reports, 'whenever something caught his eye, he would make a note, or begin sketching furiously'.

In this way, the greatest genius of the Renaissance, and perhaps of all time, was little different from those of us, some five centuries later, who carry on our person the small electronic devices by which we allow ourselves to be distracted enough to discover new things.

Leonardo was insatiably curious about the world, and one wonders, while perusing this list, which nowadays could very easily be ticked off with a few Googles or a few polite requests on social media, how much more he would have achieved had he been more single-minded and less restless in spirit and mind.

Leonardo was his own biggest critic in this regard, and in later years, he regretted 'never having completed a single work', and lamented in prayer: 'Tell me if anything ever was done. Tell me if anything was done.'

Today we know differently. We look on Leonardo as a master of his craft, not just of painting, but of science, engineering, and the dreaming-up of tools and technologies that would only come to pass many, many years later.

And the lesson we learn from his to-do list is this: if you are curious enough to want to know more, to calculate, to discover, to learn, to ask, to find out, you will get things done. Eventually.

Hey, Google, I'm home

My good friend Stephen Francis, from Brooklyn, New York, has been in town this week to revisit his old stomping grounds. 'Sunny South Africa!' he said, gazing out of the window at a late-afternoon Johannesburg deluge, shortly before stomping through the puddles to get to his car.

Stephen always kindly brings me what I like to call 'merch' from the USA, and the prize item this time around was a little electronic device, the size of a doughnut, thankfully without a hole in the middle.

It is a smart speaker, the state-of-the-artifice in home-based artificial intelligence, and what you do is place it in a convenient location in your home and talk to it. The Google Home Mini.

It sits there, quietly, waiting like a genie for your question or command, and as soon as you say, 'Hey, Google' or 'Okay, Google' – I prefer the hey version, because the okay sounds like I'm about to give it a good talking-to – it lights up the little glowing dots on its face, and it listens intently to what you have to say.

Since it's a Google device, you can ask it anything googly, such as 'what's the weather today', 'what's the population of Egypt', 'what's the traffic like to Bryanston', and 'how tall is Dustin Hoffman', and it will answer swiftly in a pleasant, perky voice that immediately made me think of Miss Moneypenny.

Unlike Siri and Alexa, the Google Assistant does not have a name, but it definitely has a personality, and it immediately ingratiated itself into my household, firstly as a novelty, and then as a physical, 3D-personification of Google itself.

The Google Home Mini, which connects to your WiFi, has

excellent voice-recognition capabilities, and has no problem comprehending South African accents of varying tones and intensities, as long as you enunciate fairly clearly and phrase your questions so as to avoid ambiguity.

For instance, when I said, as a test, 'Hey, Google, tell me about Charlie Ayers,' meaning the former executive chef of Google, who now runs a food robotics company, I got a bio of someone by the name of Charles Ayres, who is an executive chairman of Trilantic Capital Partners. Still, it was a perkily, pleasantly delivered bio, and now at least I know.

The Google Home Mini sits on a small desk in my study, behind my main desk, and I have already grown used to hey-googling questions I would previously have typed into the search bar. It's so much quicker and easier and science-fictionier.

In this way, oddly, this 21st century device, a high-tech version of the High Priestess of the Temple of Apollo at Delphi – the Oracle of Delphi – takes me right back to the ancient days of the pre-internet newsroom, where journalists would randomly shout out questions over the incessant hammering of typewriter keys.

'Anyone know what the capital of Venezuela is?' you would ask, and someone smarter than you would answer, 'Caracas.' 'How do you spell Louis Vuitton?' you would ask, and someone more fashionable than you would loudly and slowly spell out Louis Vuitton. 'What is 25 per cent of 150-million?' you would ask, and, well, silence.

But the Google Assistant is not just a fount of all knowledge. You can ask it to tell you the news of the day, or add items to your shopping list, or remind you of what's on your diary, or set a timer or alarm, or play a song or album from Google Play through its small but punchy speaker.

You can say, 'Hey, Google, remember that I put my passport in the safe,' and then, one day, when you forget, you can say, 'Hey, Google, where did I put my passport?' and you'll get your answer in a flash.

Even more smartly, the Google Home Mini can act as a hub for your smart devices – lightbulbs, thermostats, motion sensors, doorlocks, garden sprinklers – but since I don't have any of those, I can only marvel at what it one day will mean: a fully automated, intelligent home where every device will in some way be connected to the internet.

Futuristically speaking, there is nothing new about the notion of voice-activated devices ('Open the pod-bay doors, HAL'), but here at last we have a Model T version of a tomorrow in which voice will be the main platform for search, and in which we will wind up speaking more to our smart speakers than we speak to each other. It's already happening.

'Hey, Google, stop!' has become a much-shouted phrase in my household, used by other members to quieten the Home Mini when it plays my choice of music too loud.

And the other night, when Max first met the little doughnut-shaped device, the first thing he asked it was, 'Hey, Google, call Rachel a banana-head.'

'Sorry,' the Google Assistant politely replied, 'I'm not able to do that yet, but I'm learning all the time.' It's nice to have a diplomat in the house.

I'm All Shook, Because English is Lit

Today I had the great pleasure and privilege of talking to a gathering of English teachers – the correct collective noun, I believe, is a 'conjunction' – at the annual IEB English conference in Midrand.

As I told the teachers, the last time I had been in such a situation, having to deliver something resembling a speech to an academic audience, was during my matric oral exam in a previous century. And that was in front of only one English teacher. This time, there were 420 of them.

The title of my talk was 'I'm All Shook, Because English is Lit'. This caused great consternation among the Millennials in my household, who reacted with a mixture of 🙈 and 🙊 when I ran it by them.

As any parent will know, the moment a parent utters a Millennial term out loud, that term is forever cursed, and must immediately be discarded.

To make matters worse, I spent part of my talk delving into the etymology of 'on fleek', which was coined by Kayla Newman on 21 June 2014 – it is possible in the digital era to trace the origin of a word or phrase to the very moment of its Big Bang – before immediately soaring into virality and then, a few months later, plummeting in usage like the price of Bitcoin, no doubt because too many parents were using it.

I also tried, in my naïve techno-utopian way, to counter some of the popular myths about the supposedly woeful influences of smartphones and social media on the everyday usage of English.

I used a case study from Twitter, which is often criticised for encouraging informal, awkwardly constructed, typo-ridden language, but which is in fact watched over by the most ruthlessly vigilant grammarians, purists, and pernickety pedants you will find anywhere outside of an examination room.

Having said that, my experience of being taught English at school was anything but constrained and constricted by the rules, conventions, and disciplines of grammar.

That was just the foundation, the bedrock, the platform on which the teachers I was lucky to have would set us free to explore and imagine and toy around with words, emotions, and meaning.

Almost without exception, the English teachers who taught me and my peers were open-minded, progressive thinkers who were driven by a deep love of language and learning.

For my matric orals, back then, I chose 'Unjust', a long, free-verse poem by the American journalist and author, Don Marquis. 'Poets are always asking, where do the little roses go, underneath the snow,' it begins, before going on to lament that no one ever thinks to say, where do the little insects stay.

Marquis is best known for his series of tales about the cat Mehitabel, who believed herself to be a reincarnation of Cleopatra, and the typewriting cockroach, Archy, who believed that he had been a Bohemian free-verse poet in a former life.

As for Don Marquis himself, he had this to say about the process of education: 'In order to influence a child, one must be careful not to be that child's parent or grandparent.'

What he was saying, I believe, is that you should strive to be that child's teacher.

Too early for Alan Paton

Today is the 115th anniversary of the birth of the author Alan Paton, who is honoured in a Google Doodle that shows him looking pensively out of a train window at hills that are lovely beyond any singing.

The doodle quite brilliantly captures Paton's flinty, thin-lipped severity of countenance, which always seemed to be so at odds with the humanism and compassion at the heart of *Cry, the Beloved Country*.

In photographs, especially in his later years, Paton always looks like a headmaster who has called you into his office to tell you how disappointed he is in you. But if Paton was famously stern, his wife, Anne, was even more so.

She was his secretary, and she looked after his administrative matters with a vigilant, no-nonsense efficiency that left little room for fools to be suffered, gladly or otherwise.

I learned this for myself one day in the late 1980s, when I had arranged an interview with Alan Paton for a magazine story I was writing on the province that was then still known simply as Natal.

I had been warned in advance that Anne Paton was notoriously intolerant of time-wasters, dawdlers, and late-comers, so I made sure to leave plenty of time for the journey from Durban to Botha's Hill, near Pietermaritzburg, where Paton lived in sight of the Valley of a Thousand Hills.

Miraculously – these were the days before cellphones, GPS, and Google Maps – I found my way to the area, the suburb, and the house on Botha's Hill Road.

I was about 15 minutes early, so I parked outside, in the blessed shade of a big tree, and I went through my notes and questions and read, yet again, the famous opening passage of Paton's most famous book.

At about five minutes before the appointed hour, I opened the gate to the homestead, walked up the flower-scented path, listened to the sweet songs of the birds, and ... there stood Anne Paton, at the front door, arms folded, glaring at me. She unfolded her arms to glare at her watch.

'You're five minutes early!' she said. I apologised meekly, and she let me in, into the home and into the living-room of the man who one day had ridden the road that runs from Ixopo into the hills, which were grass-covered and rolling and lovely beyond any singing of it.

Hey, Siri, we need to talk

S iri, for those of you who have never been in a position to enter into a conversation with her, is the automated robotic assistant who pops up on your iPhone when you summon her with a 'hey'.

She has a soothingly modulated, convincingly human voice, with the tone of a schoolmistress who has yet to lose her patience and throw a chalkboard duster at you. The same, however, does not necessarily apply in reverse.

This is me, this morning, on the way to the airport, talking to Siri on my iPhone:

'Hey, Siri. Lanseria.'

Siri: 'Land Syria.' (Presents me with a map of Syria.)

Me, a little louder: 'LANSERIA.'

Siri: 'Gran Canaria.' (Presents me with a map of Gran Canaria, which I now know is an island in the Canary Islands.)

Me, more slowly, with heavy accent on the second syllable: 'Lan-ZE-ria.'

Siri: 'An area.' (Presents me with a Google link on How to Calculate An Area.)

Me, in rapid succession: 'Lanseria. Lanseria. Lanseria. Lanseria.'

Siri, trying to keep up: 'Rands area. Vandalia. Lan zero. I'm not sure I understand, Gus.'

Me, adjusting the algorithm a little: 'NAVIGATE TO LANSERIA.'

Siri: 'Navigate to Lanzarote.'

Me, sighing, then yelling: 'DIRECTIONS TO LANSERIA.'

Siri: 'Directions to Denver.'

Me, breathing in deeply, calming down, trying again in sudden, desperate flash of inspiration: 'Directions to airport.'

Siri: 'Looking. Which airport? Tap the one you want.' (Presents me with choice of four airports. I tap Lanseria.)

Siri: 'Getting directions to Lanseria International Airport.' (Presents me with map, takes me straight to Lanseria International Airport.)

Me: 'Thank you, Siri.'

Siri: 'Your wish is my command.'

The scary truth about artificial intelligence is that the robots we programme to serve us, are secretly programmed to programme us. Machine learning is really human learning. Once you understand this, life becomes a whole lot simpler and easier, and you can go anywhere you choose, eventually.

Beset with Durban

T he word 'beset' is typically used in a woe-is-me sense, as in: South Africa is beset with problems, challenges, and difficulties. But this week in Durban, I met a young architect named Mark Bellingan, who together with his crew (tour operator Jonas Barausse, architect Cameron Finnie, and photographer Dane Forman) is working hard to turn the meaning of the term upside-down. To make it mean: beset with promise, potential, and opportunity.

Hence, BESETdurban, which is the walking definition of a social movement, and one of the finest models of civic-minded activism I've seen in any city.

Once a month, and sometimes more, BESETdurban beckons locals and visitors alike to set foot on a journey of discovery, rediscovery, and understanding, in this balmy port city that has long sweltered in the shade of Joburg to the north and Cape Town to the south.

It is this sense of being overshadowed, of being bypassed and taken for granted, that inspired Mark and his fellow Besetters to showcase their city as it is rarely seen.

As Mark puts it, so many cool, interesting, forward-thinking and creative people come from Durban, and then they head off elsewhere; this is to prove that they haven't all left.

A BESETdurban walking tour will typically feature a guest speaker, perhaps a scientist or a surfer, an artist or an architect, an author or 'an outright Durban nerd'. Mark counts himself as a member of that species.

Lanky, witty, and laid-back, he is one of those lucky people who even as a child knew exactly what he wanted to do with his life. He grew up in Durban North, and at the age of 11, he went on a holiday visit to London with his parents.

They asked him what he most wanted to see in the Big City, expecting perhaps the Tower, Buckingham Palace, Big Ben, or Madam Tussauds. Instead he said, 'I want to see the Lloyd's Insurance building.'

Not because he wanted to work in insurance, but because the Lloyds building is a striking masterpiece of high-tech modernism, a moody, metallic, *Blade Runner*-eque sky-gouger, and Mark wanted to be an architect. So here he is today, helping to build and shape his hometown into the city of his dreams.

We met Mark at Ambassador House in Monty Naicker Street in the CBD. Once a run-down residential block, this imposing neoclassical building, dating from 1930, has been restored to its former grandeur, and given a fresh lick of exterior paint in ice-cream shades of pink and vanilla.

The building, housing office and retail space and a Curiocity backpackers lodge, is owned by Propertuity, the inner-city revitalisation firm that is best known for the Maboneng development in Johannesburg.

Then we set off on our walk. Architecture is history made visible, and in the melting-pot, the masala, the potjiekos of styles and designs, Durban comes alive through the stories of its buildings.

We popped into Pixley House, with its streamlined Art Deco façade of gold and black, and its hydroponic roof garden overlooking the bustle of Dr Pixley KaSeme Street.

We wandered into Pioneer Place, with its bold and jazzy colour scheme – violet, yellow, orange, aquamarine, pink and black – echoing the fabrics in the warren of fashion studios and sewing nooks.

We meandered by the glass-and-steel skyscrapers, the gracious Victorian City Hall, the Post Office with its high vaulted roof and light-streaming windows. Then we stopped awhile to look at a bank.

Mark stood across the road from it, on the edge of Anton Lembede Street, in the drizzle of a sudden cloudburst, and his face shone with a look of wistfulness, as if he was seeing an old friend, the flame of a love rekindled.

It was the Nedbank Building, designed by Norman Eaton in 1965: a cube at the base of a tower, shielded by a filigree sun-screen of green ceramic, flanked by slender palm trees and garlanded by vegetation.

As Mark pointed out the building's sensitivity to context and climate, its democratic use of space, allowing the lingerer or passer-by room to breathe, I began to realise that architects are as much custodians of the public imagination as poets and painters.

They build the future too; they beset it with the hope and promise of a better way of living, in cities made better for the people who live, work, and play in them.

To meander through Durban in this way is to think on your feet, to see the old Durban, the new Durban, the new-old Durban, in a whole new light, the light of knowledge and curiosity and generously shared enthusiasms.

The Jimi Hendrix of the illuminating anecdote

I saw Malcolm Gladwell in concert in Kyalami today. It felt like a concert, because in the ranks of journalists turned pop sociological thought leaders, Gladwell is the Rock Star.

He's the Jimi Hendrix of the Illuminating Anecdote, riffing on data, drenching dry texts with electric feedback, pumping up the volume on little-heard theories that deserve wider play.

Also, as I discovered while standing in a very long line at his book signing after the gig, and watching him pen squiggle after squiggle on the proffered title pages, he is, just as Jimi was, a leftie too.

I've read all of Gladwell's books, and most of his magazine articles, so I thought his presentation at the BCX Disrupt Summit – a four-hour 'masterclass', consisting of a series of talks, followed by Q & As and an interview-style chat – would be a parade of his Greatest Hits, including, you know, *The Tipping Point*, *Outliers*, and the 10 000-hour rule.

But he barely even touched on those. Much of what he said, at least from where I sat, was cut from new cloth, and even the familiar anecdotes were given a fresh spin.

For instance, the famous story of Steve Jobs, the 23-year-old geek, visiting the Xerox research lab in New York, where he first saw the computer mouse and the graphical user interface, both of which were swiftly integrated into the development of the then-fledgling Apple Lisa.

This story is usually told as a case study in the Steve Jobs School of Innovation by Appropriation – or stealing other people's ideas, as it is otherwise commonly known.

But the way Gladwell tells it, Jobs began jumping up and down with excitement when he saw the mouse and the GUI: 'This is the future of computing!' he told the Xerox engineers. 'Yes, we know,' they replied, with smug condescension.

Jobs went back to California, and the rest, as they say, is the future. The essential difference between Jobs and Xerox, says Gladwell, is that Jobs was in a hurry; the Xerox engineers were not. They felt no sense of urgency to get their innovations to market. And that is why, today, we use Macs, not Xeroxes.

Gladwell is a polymath, promiscuously interested in anything and everything, and his talks segue effortlessly from stories of little-heralded entrepreneurs to the world of high finance to leadership to sport to decisive battles of the American Civil War.

But my big 'takeaway' of the day was his elucidation of the theory of Weak Links vs Strong Links, as first postulated by the British economists Chris Anderson and David Sally.

Would you be better off in football, asked Gladwell, if you improved your best player, or your worst player? The answer, of course, is counter-intuitive. You focus on the weakest link.

Football is a game of intense interaction, and if one player fumbles a pass, the game could easily be squandered, no matter how good your star players may be.

Basketball, on the other hand, is a game of 'strong links' – as long as you have three to four 'truly amazing' players, you can get by, as Gladwell puts it, with 'one slow, lumbering white guy from Australia' in your squad.

Applied to the world of business, this means that you need to build and spread skills across your team, rather than rely on the leadership acumen of your brilliant, charismatic founder. It's at the weakest link that your company could fall apart.

Then Gladwell turned the theory to education, using the example of a school in Paris that has done away with teachers, in favour of a model of collaborative learning.

The day's problems and exercises are posted on screens, and the students work together to solve them. The strongest students help the weakest students; the weakest become stronger in the process.

This sounds to me like a dream, a vision of democracy at its most utopian. People don't need leaders – maybe they don't even need teachers – as much as they need each other.

Watching Gladwell in concert was a breath of fresh air. He is fundamentally an optimist, an advocate for the Better Angels of our nature. He reminds us that we can all be expert at something, if we just put in the hours, and he tells us that change, for the good, in politics, in business, in technology, is not just possible, but inevitable.

The Tipping Point, to use his most famous borrowed phrase, isn't just a dot on an epidemiological graph; the Tipping Point is the point at which we take charge, and hurry, like Steve Jobs did, into the tomorrow of our dreams.

Same WhatsApp group

The Pan South African Language Board has announced that the South African Word of the Year – well, two words, actually – is 'State Capture'.

This will not have come as much of a surprise to anybody, in this annus terribilis of Bell Pottinger, KPMG, assorted Eskomings and goings, and the tightly knit cabal of crooks, gangsters, and acolytes now collectively known as the President's Keepers.

But while State Capture may have earned its place at the top of the log through sheer ubiquity of usage – the research team counted 20 231 instances of the phrase in over 11 000 South African newspaper editions – the methodology was deeply flawed.

Using newspapers as a benchmark of the catchiness of a catchphrase, in the 21st century, is like using a record store in a mall as a benchmark of what sort of music people are listening to.

A far more relevant and meaningful environment for assessing the virality of a word or phrase is social media, Twitter in particular.

Here, words and phrases, whether freshly minted, repurposed, or relentlessly hashtagged into trendworthiness, take root in the common lexicon of a community that thrives on newness and novelty.

Having conducted absolutely no quantitative research into this matter at all, I would nonetheless like to propose my own candidate for South African Catchphrase of the Year. And it is: 'Same WhatsApp group'.

This is a modern equivalent of 'birds of a feather', and it is only ever used in a gleefully snide and derogatory fashion, as in, the

Boks and Bafana Bafana belong in the same WhatsApp group, after their dismal performances this weekend.

Likewise, as in Julius Malema accusing the ANC and the DA of being in the same WhatsApp group, by virtue of their joint shooting down of an EFF proposal for the nationalisation of banks.

Then there was the mysterious case of a questioning letter sent to a Parliamentary committee by the Minister of Captured Public Enterprises, Lynne Brown, at the same time as a remarkably similarly worded letter was sent to the same committee by the Black First Land First movement.

Questioned about this coincidence, the BLF's Andile Mngxitama admitted that he had 'found the questions on a WhatsApp group'. Cue plentiful mocking tweets about the Minister and the BLF being in the same WhatsApp group.

I like this phrase particularly because it taps so keenly into the social and cultural zeitgeist – who doesn't belong to a bunch of WhatsApp groups, from which, as with the Hotel California, you can check out any time you like, but you can never leave – but also because of its proud and unique South Africanness.

It is only here that we use 'same WhatsApp group' in this context, to point out the shared motives, hidden agendas, and secret alliances of people and organisations who fully deserve each other.

I wish I knew who coined this phrase, so that I could give them all due credit. But in the meantime, feel free to use it far and wide, with true South African pride, because after all, in one way or another, we're all in the same WhatsApp group.

Vaya, vaya!

Have you ever messed up an assignment at work? Really, really, messed it up, to the extent that you wanted to change your name, put on a disguise, and slink off under cover of darkness to another town, another country, another planet?

Well, here's a story that might make you feel a little better, or will at least give you the comfort of knowing that You Are Not Alone. In 1966, the great Italian director Sergio Leone was filming what would become one of the classic Westerns of all time, an epic by the name of *Il buono, il brutto, il cattivo*, or as it became internationally known, *The Good, The Bad and the Ugly*.

The movie, set during the American Civil War, was shot on location in Spain, and a climactic scene called for a railway bridge to be blown up good and proper.

The preparation was complex and intense, and the Spanish army played their part by lending dozens of soldiers to act as extras. In recognition of this, a senior officer was given the honour of igniting the blast.

The director waited patiently for the light to shift, as the camera and special effects crew stood by. The cue for the blast was the Spanish word 'vaya', which means 'go'.

As the officer awaited his signal, a crew member, urging a cameraman to get in place for the shot, said, 'Vaya, vaya!' The officer heard, thought it was the vaya he had been waiting for, and pressed the button. Ka-boomph.

The bridge blew up spectacularly, while the cameras weren't running. The crew member – who was later magnanimously re-hired – fled from the set.

Leone, watching, reacted in typically Italian fashion. 'Let's go eat,' he said. The bridge was rebuilt, and the second take, to the proper cue, is the one that made it into the movie. The moral here: Go eat. You can always blow up the bridge again later.

Drop it like Beyoncé

O ne of the oddities of the English language is the process whereby words mutate into their exact opposite meaning, like Dr Jekyll taking a swig of potion in his lab and transforming into Mr Hyde.

An example of this curious phenomenon is the simple word 'drop', which in common usage means to fall or let go. As in, 'After a drop in performance that resulted in him dropping the ball, Jantjies was dropped from the squad.'

(This is by no means intended as a reflection on Jantjies, I hasten to add; he's just the first Springbok who sprang to mind.)

So drop is almost always used in a negative sense – a drop in the value of the Rand, a drop of a major at university, a drop of a tray of puddings by a waiter in a fancy restaurant – except when it's not.

In its Dr Jekyll sense – remember, he was the good half of the two-in-one duo – drop is an upbeat, positive word, meaning its exact opposite, which is 'launch'.

As in, Beyoncé dropped her new album today, or the trailer for the new Star Wars movie just dropped on YouTube. How did this happen? When did launch become drop? Why would it be a bad thing for a singer to be dropped from a record label, but a good thing for a singer to drop a record?

I did some etymological research, and the origin of the contemporary usage seems to lie in crime movies and TV shows, where a sum of money in an envelope, or an item of sought-after merchandise, may be left at a pre-arranged point for stealthy collection. This point is known as 'the drop'. So when something of value is left at the drop for collection, it is said to have been dropped.

Thus, an album or a movie trailer is dropped, rather than launched – the suggestion being that all of us eager fans must now rush over to the drop and pick it up.

Interestingly, this informal usage has now found its way into the *Oxford English Dictionary*, the next mammoth edition of which is expected to drop by the end of this decade. But only on the internet, because of a drop in the sales of its print edition, and also because you can seriously injure yourself if you drop the OED on your foot while reaching for it on the shelf.

Don't worry, it's just a phase

This morning we had half a power failure at our home in Joburg. Our lights were working, but our plugs were not. Our neighbour across the road had the opposite problem. Their plugs were working, but their lights were not.

We logged a fault with City Power, who sent a crew out pretty quickly. They're working on it now. Apparently the problem is a 'phase problem', which is caused by people breaking into external electricity boxes and removing the fuses.

Nobody seems sure why – the theories range from the resale value of fuses, to the use of the powder contained therein as a drug or a drug-mix.

Either way, since this is not the first time this has happened, I keep thinking of that wonderful 1985 movie *Ladyhawke*, starring Rutger Hauer and Michelle Pfeiffer as doomed lovers.

The reason their love is doomed is that a spell has been cast upon them, by which Hauer is turned into a wolf during the night, and Pfeiffer is turned into a hawk during the day.

They can only be in each other's presence, as humans, briefly, at twilight. It's a very romantic story, much in the vein of *Camelot*, but without the songs.

Eventually, after logging a fault with City Power, the two lovers break the spell, and live happily ever after in electric dreams. I'm hoping the same will happen with our phase problem.

How Eskom's Prince of Darkness saved us from the bees

'The thing about a beekeeping outfit,' says Andrew Etzinger, snapping on a pair of fire-red gloves to match the headlamp on the wide-brimmed hat that crowns his face-veil, 'is that it isn't Gucci. You get a hole in it, you patch it up, and you just carry on.'

And with that, he unfolded his lightweight aluminium ladder, propped it up against the tree, and booted his way up to deal with the swarm in the hive. It was twilight, the best time of day to bother bees and find them a new home, Andrew told us, because they buzz over to the nearest white light and congregate there, rather than flitting around invisibly and stinging people.

Once, seeing off friends in the driveway, I was stung by a bee on my armpit, which is one of the least pleasant places to get stung, so I knew what he was talking about.

We found Andrew via Facebook – where else? – and he fearlessly took on the task after another beekeeper, hearing that the hive was in the crook of a tree, politely declined. But Andrew had no such qualms.

It was a complex, meticulous, painstaking job, and he popped over five twilights in a row, going about his chore with an easygoing wit and an aura of Zen calm that seemed to relax even the bees.

He told us it would have taken him five minutes to fumigate the colony, but of course we didn't want that, and nor did he, as a bee-farmer who collects his honey from hives in the Magaliesberg.

Over the course of his work, we buzzed him with a barrage of wide-eyed questions – do bees have distinct personalities? Do bats eat bees? Do bee-eaters get stung? Are bees really going extinct? – and he answered them all with patience, good grace, and an astonishing depth of expert knowledge.

It was only on the third night that I discovered why our bee-keeper's name and voice sounded so familiar to me.

From the fog of déjà vu, a bright light began to shine. In his day job, Andrew is a senior executive at Eskom, and at the height of the load-shedding crisis, he was the power utility's chief spokes-person, a calm voice of reason amidst the darkening chaos.

The Citizen at the time called him 'Eskom's Prince of Darkness', which was meant as a compliment, since he generally got on very well with the media. I asked Andrew, as he prepared to tackle the hive again, whether there was any similarity between an angry swarm of bees and a room full of journalists at an Eskom press conference. He laughed, and said, diplomatically, 'Well, you do get stung a lot.'

On one of the twilights, as he was about to put on his hat, Andrew himself got stung by an errant bee, and he brushed off the sting with barely a flinch. I would have been running around the yard, yelling for someone to fetch me a credit card. (The recom-mended method for scraping away a stinger.)

The bees have buzzed off now, thanks to Andrew, and thanks also to his expertise and the bees, I have a jar of Buffalo Thorn honey, dark, rich, and malty, from his DarlingHoney stable.

It's always a pleasure to watch someone who really knows what they're doing, going about what they do for a living, or in Andrew's case, a sideline from his busy executive role.

As he was about to call it a night one night, we asked Andrew whether beekeeping ran in his family, and he said, 'I think it skips a generation. My children don't want anything at all to do with beekeeping.'

He held out his arms in a look-at-me-in-this-beekeeping-outfit gesture. 'It's not cool,' he shrugged, and then he waved his fingers in the air. 'The thing is, you can't really Snapchat with these gloves.'

An historic occasion, unless it was a historic occasion

This week I made the mistake of using 'an historic' instead of 'a historic' in the opening sentence of a post on Facebook. Except it wasn't a mistake.

It's perfectly acceptable usage, and is favoured by, among others, *The Guardian* in the UK, and NPR and *The Wall Street Journal* in the US.

Whatever their reasons may be, mine are that the 'h' in 'historic' is so meek and stealthy that it may as well be silent, and also that 'an historic' avoids any prospect of ambiguity, since 'a historic' sounds too close for comfort to 'ahistoric', which means the exact opposite of historic.

Nonetheless, as Voltaire almost said, I will defend to the mild discomfort your right to use 'a historic' if you so choose. Both usages are equally acceptable, I argue, even as I duck to avoid the slings and arrows of outraged grammar pundits.

I am currently reading a very interesting book on grammar (yes, I read books on grammar. I'm the guy you really want to sit next to at a dinner party) called *Accidence Will Happen: The Non-Pedantic Guide to English*, by Oliver Kamm.

He's an Oxford-educated columnist and leader-writer on *The Times* of England (I think they use 'an historic' too, but I can't be sure, because they're behind a paywall) and he argues in this book for a more tolerant, flexible, and inclusive approach to the dictates and niceties of grammatical usage.

'Pedants are loud, numerous and indignant,' he writes, curiously avoiding an Oxford comma, despite having gone to Oxford.

'They are convinced that standards in English usage are falling, and they blame schools and the media for tolerating this alleged deterioration. The outcome, so these purists maintain, is linguistic barbarism, in which slang, sloppiness and text-speak supplant English grammar.' And then he adds: 'Don't believe it.'

He assures us that English is a vital, dynamic, fluid and flexible language, and that it is just as proper to go by instinct and context in its usage, as by the rules hammered into us at school. My rule of thumb on grammar has always been: if it sounds right, it's right; if it don't, it ain't.

Of course, we need rules and conventions; we can't just have grammarchy breaking out all over the place. And yet, how liberating it is to start a sentence with an 'and', or to boldly split an infinitive just because we can.

Having said all of this, I do love grammar pundits. They're my kinda people. I would far rather have a discussion, into the early hours, on whether and when one should use a semi-colon; or on why – and this is just my opinion – dashes should generally be avoided, if only because they are so impolite in the way they elbow their way into a sentence, than I would want to enter into yet another exhausting debate on the troubles of the planet, and why we are all doomed into oblivion.

So let's talk grammar and usage instead. We won't throw things, or raise our voices too loudly, but still, it will be an historic or a historic day if we ever agree on anything.

The exquisite torture of an unidentified earworm

I've had a piece of music going round and round in my head for the last few days.

A classical piece, a dark and brooding refrain, sinuously forging a trail I couldn't trace or follow. What was it? Where did it come from?

I thought I might have heard it on Classic FM, or as the soundtrack to a YouTube video, or as the subliminal theme seeping through the speakers as I browsed the shelves at Exclusive Books.

It nagged at me, like a kernel of popcorn in a tooth, and because it didn't have lyrics, I wasn't even able to google them and put myself out of my misery.

Then I was walking through the house, humming the refrain to myself, and my teenage son opened his door and said, 'Lol' – yes, he actually says 'lol' – 'Why are you humming the theme to *Game of Thrones?*'

I have never seen a single episode of *Game of Thrones*. I must have heard it, and it must have sunk in, while he was watching it on his laptop in his room.

Such is the power of popular culture, to pervade the air and invade our minds. It is a nice theme, though. And I feel much better now.

Mispronouncing the ibis

Today my good friend Denis Beckett popped over to my pozzie for a chat. As we sat in the lounge, chatting, from the kitchen came a mighty commotion. A clattering of plates, a rattling of windows, a falling of things off shelves.

I rushed in, and it was just as I suspected: a hadeda ibis had found its way into the kitchen, and had not been able to find its way out. It was not the first time this had happened, so I did not get into a flap as the ibis got into a flap.

Instead, I found an old tea-towel, approached the bird carefully, wrapped the towel around its wings as it pecked at the burglar bars, carried it outside, and set it free to fly.

I saw that Denis had been watching, from a safe distance, with what I took to be an air of high regard for my expertise. 'Not the first time we've had an ibis in the kitchen,' I shrugged. Denis looked at me quizzically, or checked me out skeef, as we like to say in South Africa.

'Do you pronounce it ibis?' he asked. 'I've always pronounced it ibis.' I could feel my heart sinking. I may be an expert in ibis-handling, but Denis, a learned scholar of the Law as well as an editor and writer of meticulous note, knows the language, in its original Latinate form as well as its contemporary variations.

I have lived in Joburg all my life, and I've always pronounced ibis with an 'i' as in 'ink', not an 'i' as in 'I'. Which, as it turns out from some emergency googling, is the correct and proper way. Who knew? Not I, as in ibis, that's for sure.

I am worried now about all the other common words that I've

been mispronouncing all my life, and all because people have been too polite to correct me. English is a strange language, with no consistency in its rules and regulations, and pronunciation often takes its cue from a consensus of quirks, rather than a set pattern of logics.

I remember in my schooldays, for example, being horrified to learn, out loud in the classroom, that the word 'science' is pronounced with a sigh in its first syllable, rather than a ski. But having been corrected in front of the class, I have not knowingly said it wrong since.

Does it matter if we say ibis or ibis? It matters not to the ibis, but that's not the point. Because from now on, to be on the safe side, I'm just going to say hadeda, and will hope that I'm saying it right.

A klutz in the gallery

'Klutz' has always been one of my favourite Yiddish words. It comes from the German 'klotz', meaning block, and it so accurately describes the bumbling, block-headed klutziness of the type of klutz who would, for instance, spill a steaming hot cup of coffee all over the pants-leg of a fellow passenger while trying to adjust their tray table on a flight, or, for that matter, bump blindly into the back of a fellow runner while glancing sidelong at another runner who had stumbled and sprawled during a Parkrun.

In both of these true-life cases, the klutz in question was me. I therefore have nothing but a deep, abiding empathy for the klutz who recently caused a computer outage that grounded 75 000 passengers and cost British Airways more than £150-million in damages at Heathrow Airport.

The finger of blame for this cataklutzmic event has now been pointed at one single klutz who pulled a plug out of a power supply in a data centre, and then, realising his human error, rapidly plugged it back in, sparking a surge that fritzed every computer in the vicinity.

It doesn't make me feel any better to learn that this was no ordinary klutz, but a highly qualified and experienced IT systems engineer, who, mercifully, has yet to be identified by anyone outside of his contracting company and the whole of British Airways.

This proves once again that anyone can be a klutz, if the timing and the circumstances are right. A couple of years ago, in the sacred space of the Museum of Modern Art in New York, I was worshipfully admiring *Water Lilies* by Claude Monet.

This series of giant canvasses by the Master of French

Impressionism spans two facing walls in the gallery, and I was lost in wonder, staring at the triptych, when I decided to snap a picture for Instagram.

I stepped back a little, and then a little more – it really is a giant canvas, and I wanted to fit it all in – when I suddenly felt the back of my leg stumbling over something soft and ropey.

'Whoa!' shouted someone, breaking the cathedral-like silence, and I managed to steady myself just before I tripped backwards over the velvet-roped barrier and went crashing right into the other wall-sized Monet.

I quickly stepped forward and took my picture, as if nothing had happened, and then I hot-footed it out of there, relieved that I hadn't gone full klutz in the glare of the most famous museum of modern art in the world.

Sure, it wouldn't have been quite as catastrophic as a systems meltdown at a major global airport hub, but it certainly would have caused me a lot of embarrassment and cost the museum a whole lot of Monet.

The haunted library of my childhood

Today I had an errand to run in Roodepoort, on the West Rand of Johannesburg. I grew up here – it's an old mining town – so I stopped out of curiosity to take a look at this building, which is 111 years old and was designed in the Victorian Gothic style. It's the town library.

The legend I learned during my childhood is that the library is haunted, and looking back now, I realise how true this was. It is haunted by pirates and princesses and dragons and explorers and wizards and ogres and elves and goblins and heroes and villains and white rabbits in a hurry looking at their watches.

I spent many hours in this building, lost in faraway lands. We stayed just a short walk away, and the primary school was just across the road, so I would wander in here with my little cardboard suitcase after school and loiter amongst the books.

Once, when I was just learning to read, I took out three books by Enid Blyton, went home and read them from cover to cover, and brought them back on the same day to exchange for fresh books.

The librarian glared at me from behind her glasses – as far as I can recall, librarians always wore glasses – and she said I couldn't possibly have read all three books in such a hurry.

I felt guilty for reading too fast, and I kept the next set of books around the house for a little longer.

Then, one day, the librarian softened her glance, looked down at me, and suggested a new book for me to read. It was *The Wonderful Wizard of Oz*, by L Frank Baum.

I remember thinking, as I raced through it, sitting up until late at night, that this was the book of books, and that I would never in my life read a better book that told a better story. But when I took it back, the librarian handed me another book, and said she was sure I would enjoy it. It was *Alice's Adventures in Wonderland*, by Lewis Carroll.

Since then, with few exceptions, every book I have read has been a better book than the one before, sometimes if only because I have gone back and re-read the books that were better.

I wanted to go into the library today, and walk up the stairs, and wander among the maze of shelves once again, but there was a notice on the door saying that the library has been closed for major renovation.

I know, in the meantime, that the ghosts will still linger, and worlds will still lie in wait in the forests of the pages. Every library in its own way is haunted, and the lessons that we learn in them stay with us forever.

Embrace your typos

The poet WH Auden once wrote a poem about Iceland. It is called 'Journey to Iceland', and it contains the following line: 'And the ports have names for the sea'.

But that wasn't how he wrote it. It was originally 'and the poets have names for the sea'. When the galley proofs came back from the printer, Auden swiftly noticed the mistake. But he left it as it was.

The misprint, on a subconscious level, added something to the poem that the poet hadn't even realised was there.

Embrace your mistypes, your autocorrects, your typos. Sometimes, in the rushed and random chaos of the universe, they can oddly work in your flavour.

The Fall of Autumn

We had an argument in the house – we only ever argue about important matters – over whether it is acceptable to use the word 'Fall' to describe the season between Summer and Winter. (Sorry, I always capitalise the seasons, but that's another argument.)

Amanda huffed and said definitely not: 'Fall should only ever be used when referring to someone tripping down the stairs.' Rachel put her hands on her hips, rolled her eyes, and said, but why not? 'Nobody talks about Autumn fashion, it's always Fall fashion.'

I said, etymologically speaking (Amanda: 'What's this got to do with insects?') that Fall was the original Old English word for the season, and that Autumn was Old French.

So the Americans, then, are the true purists, and the English probably just don't want to use the term because it reminds them of their Great Fall during the American Revolutionary War of the 18th century.

I like both words. Autumn has a hymnal sound; it hums to itself, in the mellow moments of contemplation that accompany the shifting of the seasons. And I like the vigour of Fall, the flickering fire of its colour, the way it seems to linger in the air before falling.

Autumn or Fall is my favourite season. It's a harbinger, a season in waiting, a gathering of the senses before the cold sets in. It doesn't stay for long.

It gives you notice, in the crispness of the air, the crunch of the curled leaves underfoot. And then it's gone, and Winter rushes in, and all that is left is the drift of the argument, which I like to think, at least in this case, that I won.

Hearing aids for bouviers

M any years ago, when I worked as a feature writer on the *Sunday Times Magazine* in Joburg, I took a call from a PR guy of my acquaintance.

He was the owner of a small independent agency – what one would today call a 'boutique agency', but back then was just called an agency.

He had only a few clients, but he was a good and enthusiastic pitcher, albeit sometimes difficult to understand because of his broad Scottish accent.

'I've got a great little story for you,' he said. 'Hearing aids for bouviers.' I asked him to repeat himself, and he said, 'Hearing aids for bouviers.'

I wasn't too sure about the hearing aids part, but bouviers – the big herding dogs from Flanders, formally known as Bouviers des Flandres – that sounded interesting. I wondered if they had some sort of congenital hearing problem, and I thought it might make a sweet and quirky upfront story for the mag.

I told the PR guy I would check with my editor and get back to him. 'Hearing aids for bouviers?' said my ed, not entirely convinced it was a story worth holding the front page for. 'Maybe a little upfront piece. See what else you can find out.'

So I went back to the PR guy, and said my ed was interested, but just needed a few more details … such as, how do you get the bouviers to wear their hearing aids? The PR guy didn't know what I was talking about. There was awkward silence for a moment.

'No,' he said, enunciating every syllable in perfect English, 'hearing aids for BOTH EARS.' Oh, I said, slapping myself gently on the forehead, and I went back to tell my editor, who was as disappointed as I was.

We never did run the story, but every time a PR calls to pitch, as they still sometimes do, even in the age of social media and the internet, I think about hearing aids for bouviers, and what a great little story it could have been.

Hi, I'm sorry my autocorrect spelled your name wrong

After once again almost sending an email to Legato, instead of Lerato, and to Martinis instead of Marthinus, I tweeted today about autocorrect's annoying and embarrassing propensity to autocorrect people's names.

I got some great examples from other tweeters in return.

Ho instead of Jo.
Druggie instead of Estie.
Barf instead of Brad.
Bonfire instead of Bongiwe.
Bromine instead of Bronwyn.
Trash instead of Trish.
Skype instead of Skye.
Labia instead of Kabila.
Larynx instead of Karyn.
Hen instead of Jen.
Heavier instead of Heather.
Toss instead of Ross.
Iran instead of Irna.
Zinfandel (a variety of wine) instead of Nzimande.

And this one, that the recipient in question would probably not complain about …

Faster, instead of Caster.

We are all stories, when all is said and done

There is a theory that we like to watch horror movies because we are, on the most primal level, creatures of fight or flight, and we need the occasional jolt of adrenaline to jump-start our instinct for survival.

The wiser angels of our nature are quite capable of convincing us that we are not really seeing monsters, demons, and ghosts, conjured up from the subconscious in the interplay of light and shade on a two-dimensional screen.

And yet, in the visceral shiver of cold fear that courses through our veins, we surrender, willingly, to the seductive power of the otherworld that haunts our darkest dreams.

Horror beckons us across the boundary between the real and the surreal, and we drift towards it, mesmerised, like sleepwalkers, unable to watch, unable not to watch.

And so, the other night, out of mild curiosity, I started watching *The Haunting of Hill House*, a 10-part series on Netflix, thinking it would be yet another conventional tale of a rambling, creaking old mansion that harbours secrets and a grudge.

The opening scene, all quivering violins and green mist dancing across the face of the moon, as the camera dollied towards the Gothic gables and big picture-windows, felt drenched in the clichés of the genre, but something in the voiceover narration drew me in.

'No live organism can continue for long to exist sanely under conditions of absolute reality,' intoned the voice. 'Even larks and katydids are supposed, by some, to dream. Hill House, not sane, stood by itself against the hills, holding darkness within.'

That, as it turns out, is the opening paragraph of Shirley Jackson's 1959 novella, *The Haunting of Hill House*, regarded by many, most notably Stephen King, as one of the greatest works of supernatural fiction ever written.

But the original tale serves only as a harbour for the series, which pulls up anchor and sets sail for a faraway place and time.

Something terrible and unexplained happens within the walls of the not-sane Hill House one night, we learn; something that drives a father, his face ashen with dread, to gather his brood of five children, hasten them down the grand baronial staircase, and into a station-wagon, leaving the mother mysteriously behind and alone.

Then the journey leads us to the present moment, some two-and-a-half decades down the road, when the siblings, now supposedly settled into their separate suburban lives, in the soft comforts of approaching middle-age, are revealed to be not settled at all.

They are haunted, still, by the events of their childhood, not only by the shifting, floating, scream-faced figures that visit them at night, but by the greater monsters, ghosts, and demons of the mind: addiction, loss, repression, bitterness, madness, and regret.

The Haunting of Hill House, its narrative shifting back and forth in time, is really a story of a family in dysfunction, of the psychic toll of fractured relationships and memories that won't go away.

There are spectres and apparitions aplenty in the series – the most terrifying, for me at any rate, being a tall, bowler-hatted figure, feet floating above the ground, knocking on the bedroom floor with a cane – but there is hardly any blood and gore, nor any books of arcane spells or priests with holy water, making house calls. It's not that kind of horror story.

It's the much scarier kind – subtle, elegant, whispering, soul-shivering, and the line that stays with me, that really made me catch my breath, is this, from a mother to her child: 'When we die, we turn into stories. And every time someone tells one of those stories, it's like we're still here, for them. We're all stories in the end.'